ROBERT WOLFF'S
BOOK OF GREAT WORKOUTS

ROBERT WOLFF'S
BOOK OF GREAT WORKOUTS

Everything You Need to Know to Vary Your Routine and Keep You Motivated

ROBERT WOLFF, PH.D.

CB
CONTEMPORARY BOOKS

Library of Congress Cataloging-in-Publication Data

Wolff, Robert, Ph.D.
    Robert Wolff's book of great workouts : everything you need to
know to vary your routine and keep you motivated / Robert Wolff.
        p.   cm.
    ISBN 0-8092-9769-8
    1. Physical fitness.   2. Exercise.   I. Title: Book of great
workouts.   II. Title.
GV481.W655   2001
613.7—dc21   00-55502
                                     CIP

Cover design by Todd Petersen
Cover and interior photographs copyright © Michael Neveux
Interior design by Hespenheide Design

Published by Contemporary Books
A division of the McGraw-Hill Companies
4255 West Touhy Avenue, Lincolnwood (Chicago), Illinois 60712-1975 U.S.A.
Copyright © 2001 by The Creative Syndicate, Inc.
Printed in the United States of America
International Standard Book Number: 0-8092-9769-8
01 02 03 04 05 06 VL 19 18 17 16 15 14 13 12 11 10 9 8 7 6 5 4 3 2 1

Also by Robert Wolff

*Bodybuilding 101: Everything You Need
to Know to Get the Body You Want*

CONTENTS

"What should I do today?" Ever ask yourself that question when you're feeling unmotivated to work out? Geez, I sure have. We all have at one time or another.

Over the years, friends have told me they always enjoy training with me because they never know what kind of workout we'll do next. It's true. It's a real hoot to just make stuff up as you go along, to always try new things and see what works. A lot of times, we'll have dud workouts. Other times, they are so incredible that we don't want them to end.

I've picked out some of the best workouts that have consistently worked well and put them together in this book. With *Robert Wolff's Book of Great Workouts*, you will save hours, months, and years of time trying to find something different that might work. I think you'll be amazed at just how quickly you'll notice the change in how you look and feel.

Probably one of the biggest things that frustrate people who work out is the ups and downs of motivation. One workout they're totally stoked and feel like going all out, while the next workout they feel like they're dragging a ball and chain around the gym.

One big thing I observed, not only in myself but in others who've trained with me, was how excited we became whenever we tried something new and different. Whether a new exercise or workout, as long as it was different, we looked forward to doing it.

This got me thinking. It's just human nature to want something to look forward to. Being surprised keeps us positive, happier, and definitely motivated. And our lives are much more exciting when we have a lot of things to look forward to. The more little things we have, like new and different workouts, the more little excitements we feel, the happier we become. Having said all that, by the time you finish this book, you'll be so happy, you won't be able to contain yourself.

In the pages that follow, you will find some tips, exercises, workouts, and advice that can change your body—how you look and feel—in a big way, more quickly than you may have thought possible.

You'll find me repeating things throughout the book, but it's for good reasons. Whenever we learn something new, it usually takes either repeating the new action over and over, or hearing again or rereading key points to remember, in order for it to stick.

If I were training you, each time we would begin your workout—at least until you got the hang of it—I would go over with you what we did together on your last workout, to reinforce and help you better remember what you learned. For example, I might say to you, "OK, the last workout we did the incline chest press and we adjusted the bench angle to 25 degrees. I had you do 10 reps with elbows up at shoulder level when you lowered the weights to your chest. Remember how you felt them really stretch your chest? Incredible, wasn't it? And then I had you rest about 25 seconds before you did your next set. Then we moved to the close-hand push-ups with your feet elevated on a bench where you . . ."

Since I can't physically be with you as you read this book or in the gym with you when you're working out, I've found it very effective to repeat important points—whether they concern training, nutrition, or motivation—so that all of this great information you're about to learn will be absorbed by your brain as water is by a sponge.

I would like you to look at the workouts you're about to learn as starting points for *your own best workouts*. You and I differ in our training goals, body types, levels of experience, motivation, genetics, and so many other things. But we're very similar in wanting to find great workouts that will give us great results lasting a lifetime. I can think of no better place for us to start than right here, right now, with this book.

ACKNOWLEDGMENTS

Many thanks to all of the great people who made this book a reality, including

You, the reader, to whom this book is written. May it give you many years of great workouts and help you whenever you want to change the way you look and feel.

Matthew Carnicelli, Katherine Hinkebein, and everyone at Contemporary Books.

Michael Neveux for the great photography. Special thanks to your staff for all their help.

PART I

Understanding the Fundamentals

Getting Started

One of the most enjoyable things about working out is the joy you get from seeing and feeling your body change. The problem is, after a few years of working out many of us reach a plateau where the great results slow down and stop. This has caused many people to quit when they didn't need to. In fact, if they only had changed their workouts and the way they trained, they could have kept progressing year after year. It's really that simple.

In a few chapters, we're going to get into some great new workouts for you. But before we do, I will give you a few great tips. For the first tip you'll need a pen and notebook because the following workout log can save you much time and frustration and really help you reach your goals.

KEEP A TRAINING LOG

A Reminder of Just How Far You've Come

Keeping a training log, a detailed record of your workout routines, is a great way to help you get past sticking points. A log will enable you to formulate new and varied routines—either from the ones in this book or your own—so you can enjoy great training success for many years.

It's simple: just keep a record of every workout you do. This is important for a number of reasons:

1. A log gives you a good indication of your training progress. If you're getting stronger, your body will show it.
2. A training log gives you precise information about which exercises and workouts are working and which aren't.
3. This valuable feedback allows you to keep the exercises and workouts that work for *your* body and eliminate the ones that don't.
4. You can refer to your training log at any time and formulate new routines from the set, rep, and weight combinations that work best for you.

Over the years, many people have used training logs with fabulous success. Think about it: can you remember a workout you did four months ago that got your legs incredibly sore? You could if you looked it up in your training log.

EXPERIMENT, EXPERIMENT, EXPERIMENT

It's All About What Works Best for You

The second tip I want to share with you is the need for you to experiment. If you want workout success, you must do the exercises and workouts that *your* body responds best to. That means doing your own thing. For example, try doing numerous exercises for each muscle group. You'll find that some will work well and others won't do diddly. Instead of taking someone else's word

for it and copying his or her routine, go to the gym and find out for yourself what works and what doesn't.

Often an exercise won't produce results until you change the angle of the movement. Then it becomes an incredibly effective growth and strength producer.

You wouldn't have discovered and benefited from this, however, unless you took the time to test every element of the exercise. You must search for any and every part of an exercise that works for you and you alone.

USING WHAT YOU'VE LEARNED

This Is When It Gets Fun

The third tip for workout success is using what you've learned. This means taking those exercises and workouts that work best for you and applying them in ways that will give you great results year after year.

If you haven't already, you're going to find that your body can quickly become stale if you do the same thing all the time. Can you say *boring*? The trick is to keep your body off-guard. How? By using different combinations of exercises, sets, and reps; using different workouts and weights; and increasing intensity. Instead of doing only straight sets, mix it up and do supersets (two exercises for opposing bodyparts, e.g., triceps and biceps), and tri-sets and giant sets (multiple exercises performed back-to-back for the same bodypart).

You might decide to pick one exercise for one bodypart and do 10 sets of 10 reps. How about doing two different exercises for a bodypart and doing a heavy or light superset? For example, do heavy standing barbell curls for 8 reps and then immediately do a set of dumbbell hammer curls for 12. This combo is a killer!

Always do something different, such as thumbs-up curls for biceps.

The exercise variations are endless and so are your workout possibilities. The only thing to hold you back is your imagination. If you're serious about getting the most from your training on a long-term basis, you've got to find the best exercises for you, mix them up regularly, write these workouts down in your training log, and refer to the log often in order to formulate new exercise routines.

Now, I can give you all the great exercises and workouts you want, but remember that the most important reason to work out is to have fun. The health and appearance benefits are only secondary. Enjoy your workouts. Enjoy how wonderful your body feels after a good workout. Most of all, enjoy the priceless and precious gift called your life! Working out isn't something you *have* to do. It should be something that you *want* to do.

2

The Importance of Fuel

Nutrition has become very important to people. Thankfully, people today are more informed about nutrition and are better able to separate the real truth from the real hype than they have been in the past. Yet, with so many experts telling you that you need this supplement or that diet to achieve optimal performance, nutrition can get confusing. I hope to clear up some of that confusion.

My philosophy about nutrition is simple. Eat a good balance and wide variety of fresh and nutritious foods from all the food groups, cut back on junk foods, drink *a lot* of water, supplement your diet with a good multivitamin/mineral and extra vitamin C, and take advantage of time windows of opportunity—after your training, sport, or activity—to refuel your body for your next workout.

Don't get caught up in supplements, thinking they will dramatically increase your performance. Supplements are not drugs, and they don't produce druglike effects. Over the years, I've met and worked with many of the world's best bodybuilders,

fitness athletes, and weekend warriors who took their training, sports, and activities seriously, and some conclusions can easily be made regarding any other supplements besides vitamins and minerals. They are

1. Supplements are just that: a supplement to an already good, healthy, nutritious, and balanced diet.
2. Supplements work for some people but not nearly as well for others.
3. Many people for whom supplements work report *minimal* differences in performance.
4. For the even smaller number of those who experience noticeable changes in performance, those gains cost a lot of money and are short-term at best.
5. Supplements are expensive.
6. You have to take them often and in high dosages to get the incredible results reported in magazines.
7. Save your hard-earned cash!

IT'S ALL ABOUT UNDERSTANDING YOUR INCREDIBLE ENERGY MACHINE

Before getting into some guidelines about what and when to eat, you need to understand how your body uses the foods you eat for energy and power. When you're in the middle of your workout, favorite sport, or activity, whether indoor or ourdoor, you don't want anything slowing you down. Let's first talk about power and fuel for your incredible machine.

Pure anaerobic (without oxygen) power can be used for about one minute, meaning you can train at levels that are greater than your body's ability to supply oxygen to your muscles. For activities longer than one minute, your body kicks in the use of aerobic (with

oxygen) power and must have a continuous supply of oxygen. This is especially true for activities longer than five minutes. During exercise, however, both energy systems work together to supply your body with the energy it needs.

Think of the foods you eat as the fuel for energy, and the anaerobic and aerobic systems as the vehicles that deliver that fuel to your body. Of all the foods you eat, carbohydrates are used the most quickly by the body. The body breaks down carbohydrates into glucose. Glucose is stored in the muscles and liver as glycogen—the fuel your body will use for the workouts and activities you like to do.

When oxygen is not available for the body to use, glucose is the next choice. If you're exercising anaerobically—for example, weight training—then glucose is converted to pyruvate, which becomes lactic acid. Too much lactic acid can adversely affect your performance by affecting the abilities of

For great results, fuel your body with nutritious foods each day.

your muscles to contract and your body to produce energy.

Because of this, your body's anaerobic power can only fuel your muscles for about a minute or so before the aerobic system takes over. Then the lactic acid production is reversed. The lactic acid is converted back into pyruvate and used by the muscles as fuel, with any excess lactic acid channeled back to the liver and processed back into glucose.

Making sure your body gets plenty of oxygen is crucial to your success in getting the most out of whatever workout or activity you do. This is especially true when it comes to energy, because your body can use glucose better when it doesn't have to be converted to lactic acid. In fact, your body is able to break down glucose aerobically to produce almost *20 times more* energy than when glucose has to be converted into lactic acid.

Many people believe that if they keep their amino acid intake high, then their energy also will be high. Not so. The body will not be provided with energy from protein (amino acids are the building blocks of protein) or fat unless the body has oxygen. And if the body doesn't get enough oxygen, it will use glucose.

YOUR BODY AND WORKOUT TRAINING DURATION

Many people wonder why they feel they can train for long periods, yet their bodies won't allow it. Think of it like this: *you can either train hard or train long, but you can't do both.*

When your training exceeds 90 minutes, the fuel of your muscles (glycogen) becomes more depleted. Your body's ability to use oxygen is the big factor that will ultimately determine how long and intensely you'll be

able to work out or train in your favorite activity or sport. The good news is that your oxygen use and uptake can be optimized with training over a period of time, so just be patient.

Most people don't realize that the body will use its most dominant food source as its energy source. For example, if you eat a lot of fat, your body will use more fat for fuel; if you eat a lot of carbohydrates, then your body will use carbohydrates as glycogen for the fuel source. But both are not used equally efficiently or effectively.

You must have a balance of nutrients. Too much fat means you're eating fewer carbs. And not eating enough carbs adversely affects muscle fuel (glycogen), thereby limiting your ability to perform exercise at peak levels and over long periods of time.

Many people have found that to keep energy levels high, they must eat 4 to 7 grams of carbohydrates (try to get roughly 50 percent from fast-burning simple sugars such as fruit, juices, honey, etc., and the other 50 percent from slow-burning complex carbs such as vegetables, beans, grains, pasta, legumes, brown rice, etc.) per pound of bodyweight (e.g., a 175-pound person would eat 700 to 1,225 grams of carbohydrates per day). You must experiment to find the best ratio for you.

CARBOHYDRATE LOADING FOR PERFORMANCE

For years, especially in the bodybuilding and fitness world, the old rationale used to be to take one week and radically decrease your carbs for the first three or four days, then slowly introduce carbs back into your system. The theory was that the body would be so depleted from the previous three or four days of low carbs that it would "soak up and store" the carbs coming back into the body. For some, this worked fine. For most, however, it was hit or miss; they could not accurately predict how their bodies would respond. Yet many swore by it because they didn't know better.

However, what research has found is that endurance-based training causes the synthesis of muscle glycogen by means of something called glycogen synthase, which is the enzyme that helps glycogen storage. That means while carb loading, increasing your carb intake and cutting back on your weight training at the same time is the way to store more muscle glycogen or workout fuel. The more muscle fuel, the less chance you will get pooped out.

Will carbohydrate loading work for everybody? Sorry. There seems to be a correlation between your amount of endurance-based training and the effectiveness of carb loading. In other words, if you're not endurance training (e.g., you're only weightlifting), then carb loading won't change your muscles' ability or capacity to store more muscle fuel (glycogen). However, if you've been training hard and much of that training has been endurance-based, then your body's ability to store muscle glycogen can be nearly two times as much as someone who hasn't been training like you, and that's without carbohydrate loading!

One of the goals for many workout enthusiasts is to "teach" their body to become better fat-fuel users. If that's important to you, then how do you do it? One of the best ways is to make sure your training sessions last at least *one hour* or more. This also means changing the way you train. Keep in mind that it takes roughly 25 minutes of endurance exercise for your body to switch to the fat-burning mode.

And don't exercise too intensely. If you do, your body will switch from fat burning to muscle fuel (glycogen) burning. Always remember that the more your body can effectively use fat, the less it will use muscle glycogen.

WHAT ABOUT PROTEIN?

Without a lecture on protein, here are some basics to keep in mind.

- If you consider yourself to be a hard-training workout athlete, you're going to need more protein than someone who doesn't train as hard as you. How much? A good range would be 0.7 to 1.3 grams per pound of bodyweight per day.
- Many people still believe the myth that the body can use only 20 to 50 grams of protein at a time. But scientists and researchers I've spo-

Your body needs protein, slightly more if you're a hard-trainer, but don't overdo it.

ken to say they've yet to see a conclusive study that proves this. That means your body type, age, metabolism, genetics, activity, and intensity level all determine how much protein your body will need at any given time. So experiment and find what's best for you.

- If your body is able to use sufficient muscle glycogen and fat fuel, then the fuel used and needed from protein could be less than 20 percent of your body's daily requirements.

- Remember that carbohydrates are protein sparing. That's a good thing, because you want all the protein used by your body for tissue repair and recovery.

- Great protein sources would be lean meat, skinless chicken and turkey, fish, egg whites, nonfat dairy, and skim milk powder.

- Many athletes say you need supplements, especially amino acids. But would you believe, you can more effectively and cheaply get the aminos you need from the foods you eat? The following basics may open your eyes.

- First of all, keep in mind that over 90 percent of the amino acids from the foods you eat (animal and vegetable) are used by your body. Consider that the average amino acid capsule supplement has roughly 200 to 500 milligrams (some much less) of amino acids, whereas a food such as only two ounces of fish, chicken, or beef, has about 14 grams of protein, or nearly 14,000 milligrams—not 200 to 500 milligrams like the amino acid capsules—of amino acids. And the added bonus is that these amino acids are released slowly over time by the body. Let's do a little eye-opening math.

1. The average amino acid supplement contains 200 to 500 milligrams of amino acids per capsule. For comparison purposes, we'll say each capsule equals 500 milligrams of amino acids.

2. Let's also say that the average bottle contains 100 capsules and costs 20 dollars.

3. That's 100 capsules × 500 milligrams of amino acids per capsule, which comes out to be 50,000 milligrams or 50 grams of amino acids per bottle.

4. At 20 dollars a bottle, that comes out to be 40 cents per gram (20 cents per capsule), and you would have to take two capsules (40 cents' worth) to get one gram of amino acids. Still with me? Good, it's about to get interesting . . .

5. To give your body the 7 grams of amino acids that you could get from just a one-ounce piece of fish, chicken, or beef, you would have to take 14 amino acid capsules. And those 14 capsules would cost you $2.80 (i.e., 14 × 20 cents/capsule = $2.80).

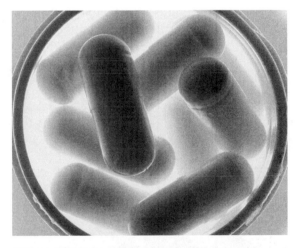

Why spend $2.80 for supplements when you can get the same amount of protein in food for 25 cents?

6. To get the same amount of amino acids from just a one-ounce piece of fish, chicken, or beef (and let's assume a per-pound price of $4.00) would cost you . . . are you ready for this? About 25 cents. That's right, just 25 pennies.

7. So you decide: do you want to fork out $2.80 for the amino acid supplement capsules or spend just a measly 25 cents and get the same benefits from food?

- The bottom line: save your money and eat a good diet, and you'll get all the nutrients you need and much more.

- And regardless of where you get your amino acids, from either food or supplements, always remember that the body ultimately uses the acids in the same way. So if you take too much, it will either go down the toilet or the extra calories (beyond what your body needs) will be stored as fat.

WHAT ABOUT OTHER SUPPLEMENTS?

I've been a big believer, along with many other athletes, in sticking with

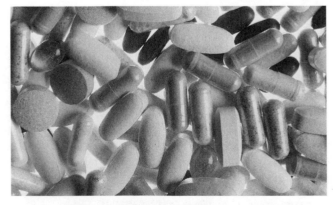

Vitamin C supplements are beneficial, but save your money—the cheapest works just as well as the most expensive.

the basics: a good multivitamin/mineral supplement with perhaps additional antioxidant supplementation like extra vitamin C. My personal supplement regimen consists of one multivitamin/mineral and 1,000 milligrams of vitamin C twice a day, at breakfast and dinner. I'm always healthy, full of energy and plenty of power, and my cholesterol ranges from 108 to 143—pretty cheap insurance.

A few years ago, I had the unique privilege of interviewing the late Dr. Linus Pauling twice, the only man in history to win two Nobel prizes, both unshared. Quite a brilliant man. Over the years, Pauling has had his share of critics for his outspoken views on many subjects, especially his promotion of vitamin C. During one of our talks, Pauling told me that studies have shown how added vitamin C helps reduce cholesterol (for those with high cholesterol), elevates it to healthy levels for those with abnormally low cholesterol, and helps prevent heart disease. All these things from simply supplementing one's diet with extra vitamin C. And don't buy the expensive kind. Pauling said you don't need it; the cheapest works just as well.

If you're a person who works out hard and wants the best results, definitely watch your iron intake, especially if you're a woman. Your body needs iron to form hemoglobin, which transports oxygen in your blood and sends it to your tissues. When your body doesn't have enough hemoglobin, your muscles don't get the oxygen they could use and your performance drops. Women need about 15 milligrams of iron a day, and men need about 10 milligrams. The best sources are animal products (about one milligram per ounce), since the iron is more effectively absorbed than that of vegetable-based sources.

Giving your body the proper nutrients doesn't need to be confusing or expensive. It may help to remember this nutrition maxim: Get enough protein, carbohydrate, fat, thiamine, calcium, iron, niacin, riboflavin, and vitamins C and A in your diet, and there's a good chance you'll get all the other extra nutrients your body needs. You get these nutrients from eating a good variety of meats, vegetables, fruits, dairy, and grains.

WHAT ABOUT WATER?

The majority of people don't get enough water. It seems like the only gauge they use to decide whether or not to give their body water is thirst. Wrong. By the time you feel thirsty, you've lost significant amounts of fluid, which will already be affecting your performance.

I've found that the more water you drink, the better. Not only does your body need water to cleanse its system, but water also aids in fat metabolism. And not having enough water can adversely affect your workouts.

Muscle is primarily composed of water, and a loss of fluid volume in muscle cells negatively affects power and output. For example, some research has shown that for every 1 percent of weight your body loses from dehydration (i.e., loss of water), your peak performance can drop by 10 percent.

For the average nontraining person, I recommend a *minimum* of 8 to 10 eight-ounce glasses of water per day. If you're hitting it pretty hard, then raise that amount to over 120 ounces. A rule of thumb that many athletes follow is to *drink the same amount in ounces of water to match their bodyweight* (i.e., a 175-pound man would drink 175 ounces of water). Of course, the rather simple way to check and see if you're

Don't wait until you're thirsty to drink water. Keep your body hydrated all day long.

getting enough water is to check your urine. If it's not clear, then you need to drink more.

WHAT ABOUT ELECTROLYTES?

Physical activity causes our bodies to lose electrolytes. And one of the best ways to replace those electrolytes—besides buying a complete sports drink—is to get them from foods you probably already eat. For example, to replace sodium and chloride, add a little extra salt to your food. To replace potassium, you can't go wrong with fruits like oranges and bananas.

WHAT TO EAT BEFORE EXERCISE

We're all different, so there's no single tried-and-true piece of advice that will work for everyone. Experiment. Over the years, many have believed that eating a meal loaded with complex carbohydrates (like pasta) the night before you train loads the body with plenty of energy for the next day. Others say the meal roughly two hours before your activity is what makes the difference. Personally, I've found it to be a combination of both *plus* two other variables: the amount of activity performed the week before and the overall composition of the diet for that week.

Interestingly, I've found that if I worked out hard for at least three or four days that week, the regular and extra calories ingested during my meals seemed to be primarily used for recuperation, repair, and growth from the previous exercise I put my body through, with little left over for addi-tional weight training, sports, or activity demands. However, on the weeks that I cut back on the intensity of my workouts and I kept my complex carbohydrate intake at roughly 50 percent, protein at 35 percent, and fat at 15 percent, I found that my body had plenty of energy and endurance for whatever workout or anything else I was doing.

Again, you, me, and everyone else will differ somewhat in how our bodies respond to foods and various ratios of carbohydrates, protein, and fats. If you're looking for hard-and-fast rules that work for everybody all the time, you're not going to find them.

Think of your body as a specially built engine. While most car engines

If you want a great looking and feeling body, remember this: Eating clean will help you stay lean.

run on gas, each engine will still run and respond differently to the octane of fuel, spark plugs, pistons, size of the engine, crankshaft, exhaust tuning, timing, and weight of the vehicle being powered. Your body is the same. Your height, weight, build, genetics, metabolism, previous and current conditioning, food choices, nutrient ingestion schedule, liquid consumption, macro and micro nutrient balance, and your body's ability to effectively use nutrients all play big factors in determining what your body needs and responds best to.

But no need to worry. I can give you some good guidelines to help you build a balanced foundation for energy, power, and good health from which you can tweak the variables to make your engine run at its best.

Just like with your workouts, eat something different each day.

CREATING A FUN, ENJOYABLE, HEALTHY, COST-EFFECTIVE, DOABLE, AND POWER-PACKED EATING PLAN

1. I suggest eating small meals throughout the day about three to four hours apart. Small meals won't overtax your body's ability to digest and assimilate the nutrients and will allow it to better use those nutrients with minimal waste. Small meals keep your blood sugar levels stable all day and give your body the ratio of proper nutrients it needs at the time and amounts it can optimally use.

2. Eat clean to be lean. For the most part, a leaner athlete (within reason) can be a more effective athlete. Excess bodyfat slows you down; fat takes up space and is not living tissue like muscle.

3. Lean muscle tissue is living tissue (it needs nutrients to feed it), and the more you have—within reason —the more of those nutritious

foods you can eat. Frequent smaller meals, along with the extra calories your lean tissue needs, help create a metabolic boost that allows your body to burn calories more efficiently. Some people say all of these things help their bodies to burn bodyfat more effectively. Take the best of both worlds: eat more calories, lose more fat.

4. Always keep in mind, however, that the biggest factor in losing bodyfat is *the total amount of calories you eat in a day versus the total number of calories you burn in a day.*

5. Forget ratio of nutrients, nutrient timing, and all that other stuff. If you eat more food than you can use, you will get fat—end of story.

TIPS FOR BREAKFAST

- Always have a good breakfast and never miss this meal.
- Choose a different kind of breakfast every day.

- Always have a glass of water upon waking and about 20 to 30 minutes before a meal so it won't interfere with digestion.
- During the meal, sip on only enough water to help you swallow the food. Drinking too much water with the meal tends to dilute important stomach acids needed to break down nutrients from the food.
- Some great breakfast choices include
  - Cottage cheese (nonfat or low-fat) and fruit
  - Yogurt mixed with muesli, bran, or high-fiber cereal
  - Eggs with grapefruit and unbuttered whole-grain bread
  - High-fiber and low-fat cereal with skim milk
  - Fresh juice with bagels
- Oatmeal mixed and cooked with skim milk, honey, and sliced banana, fortified with extra skim-milk powder

TIPS FOR LUNCH

- Some great lunch choices include
  - Dark-green salad with tuna (in spring water), turkey, or chicken, and a piece of fruit
  - Tuna or egg-white salad (made with nonfat mayo, sweet relish, chili powder, celery salt, and celery) with nonfat or low-fat whole-grain crackers, and a piece of fruit
  - Bagel with low-fat chicken or tuna salad spread, and a piece of fruit

You have many choices for breakfast—try something new.

Create your own fun and great-tasting meals with the tips in this book.

TIPS FOR DINNER

- Some great dinner choices include
  - Fish, lean beef, skinless chicken, or turkey
  - Pasta (with red sauce, low-fat white sauce, or plain)
  - Dark-green, leafy and fibrous vegetables
  - White fibrous vegetables (cauliflower)
  - Richly colored vegetables (tomatoes, squash, peppers, etc.)

TIPS FOR SNACKS

- Some great snack choices include
  - Fruit
  - Celery, carrots
  - Popcorn (no butter)
  - Rice cakes with applesauce
  - Beef or turkey jerky
  - And don't forget about bagels. A study by Ball State University revealed that bagels provide the same amount of carbohydrates as energy bars. Why pay a dollar or two for an energy bar when you can get a bagel for about 20 to 40 percent less?

Refueling your body right after your workout can make a big difference in your fitness success.

WHAT TO EAT AFTER EXERCISE

Researchers believe that after you work out, a critical window opens for refueling your body's muscle glycogen that was used during your workout. Some research has shown that the body will store more glycogen *twice as effectively* shortly after exercise (within about 40 minutes) than at other times throughout the day when there was no exercise. Other research has shown that the body will store as much as *two times* the amount of glycogen from sucrose and glucose than from fructose.

Determine which after-workout refueling method works best for you.

CAFFEINE OR NO CAFFEINE?

Some athletes swear by it. Here are the quick findings:

- Caffeine may help the body burn fat and use fewer carbohydrates.
- Caffeine raises mental awareness and diminishes fatigue.
- Caffeine may intensify muscle contraction by improving the muscle's use of calcium, potassium, and sodium.

3

Training the Endomorph

We live in a world where one size fits all and one kind of advice should be good for everyone. But this is a mistake, especially when it comes to our bodies. Knowing your body type and how to train it can put you on the fast track to great results.

So, what's your type? Here are the three basic body types:

- Endomorph—characterized by soft musculature, short neck, round face, wide hips, and an inclination toward heavy fat storage
- Ectomorph—characterized by long arms and legs, short upper torso, long and narrow feet and hands, narrow chest and shoulders, very little fat storage, and long, thin muscles
- Mesomorph—characterized by a large chest, long torso, great strength, and solid musculature

As a rule, no one is of just one particular body type. We tend to be combinations of all three. But each of us leans toward one of the three types, and knowing how these different

body types respond to training and diet can help you reach your workout, body, and health goals more quickly.

One of the questions asked most by those who work out is "How should I train?" As you can imagine, coming up with one answer is a challenging task. We all have different body types, goals, levels of experience, motivation, training time, nutritional needs and habits, and other factors. Since what works best for one person may not work for another, I will give you some practical training advice based upon one particular aspect: body type. Let's begin by discussing training for the endomorph—the kind of body that tends to be heavyset.

And while many of the exercises I discuss will work for any build, it's *how* you do them that can make all the difference with regard to your body type.

Endomorphs may be heavier than other body types, but they can pack on muscle and strength fast.

THE ENDOMORPH TRAINING PHILOSOPHY

Intensity and Aerobics

Endomorphs typically have a higher than normal percentage of bodyfat. On the plus side, many endomorphs are blessed with a big and wide bone structure. Weight gains come easily, while losing bodyfat can be much more difficult.

Often, the weight endomorphs gain stays right where they don't want it: on the abs, waist, and buttocks. As endomorphs begin weight training, they tend to gain size—much of it muscle—fairly quickly. The muscle, however, often remains hidden under layers of fat. Ironically, an endomorph's body can be hard as a rock, yet achieving a good degree of definition always remains just out of reach.

Many endomorphs, because of their advantageous bone size and ability to put on muscle quickly, train with heavy weights and low reps. This is often a mistake. *An endomorph should train with moderate poundage, high intensity, minimal rest between sets, and more frequent workouts.* The goal is, through diet *and* training, to amp up the metabolism and make the muscle burn and carve new cuts and definition.

Another very important training element is cardiovascular fitness. Far too many endomorphs simply do weight training and nothing else. That's another big mistake. An endomorph will never achieve the degree of leanness desired unless he or she has a good diet and trains the cardiovascular system at least three times per week. Excellent cardiovascular workout choices include brisk walking, the stair stepper, stationary or regular biking, racquet sports, hiking, and walking on the treadmill.

Be sure to do your cardiovascular training in your target heart zone, a range that depends on your age. To compute your range per minute, subtract your age from 220 and multiply that number by 0.6 and 0.7. After a five-minute warm-up, exercise in your target heart zone for 15 to 20 minutes, then cool down for 3 to 5 minutes.

THE ENDOMORPH WORKOUT

As always, keep the workouts fun. That means change your training program regularly, e.g., every second or third workout. Then follow these tips:

- Take three to five exercises that work well for each bodypart, and use them as your pool of exercises to choose from for each workout.
- Choose two to three different exercises for each bodypart from the pool of exercises for each workout.
- Do one basic movement (e.g., incline dumbbell press for chest) and one to two isolation movements (e.g., dumbbell flyes, pec deck, or cable crossovers).

- Decrease your rest time between sets to no more than 60 seconds.
- Keep your reps in the 9 to 12 range for upper body and the 12 to 25 range for legs and calves.
- In each workout vary the rest times, reps, sets, and weights. Keep your body constantly off-guard.
- Train abdominals at the beginning of your workout.
- Do no more than 8 sets per bodypart.
- Work out on a split-training system. For example, on Monday work chest and arms, on Tuesday work legs, and on Wednesday work back and shoulders. Thursday is a day off from weight training, and you repeat the training schedule again on Friday.

One of the most important training tips for the endomorph to keep in mind is training intensity. The endomorph must constantly keep the training intensity high. Make your body work harder by working smarter, using the preceding guidelines. Keep the workouts fresh and exciting, and don't allow yourself to fall into a rut. Do something different each workout.

4

Training the Ectomorph

If you're an ectomorph, building muscle mass can be quite a challenge. Ectomorphs tend to be lean, and putting on size may seem to take forever if you're not following a solid game plan. With proper guidelines, however, you can get to your workout goals quickly. These tips should help:

- Do the basic exercises that emphasize power movements for building mass. Exercises like squats, deadlifts, presses, chin-ups, rows, and barbell curls are excellent mass builders.
- Keep your reps in the 6 to 8 range and sets in the 8 to 12 range. Be sure to give your body enough rest between sets so you can continue to lift heavy, with good form, to induce muscle-fiber stimulation for growth.
- Your training goal should be less volume and more intensity. Train no more than three days per week in order to give your body sufficient time for recuperation, repair, and growth. The Monday–Wednesday–Friday workout schedule is ideal.

LET'S TALK NUTRITION

Nutrition is a big factor for the ecto-morph in gaining weight and muscle mass. If you're ectomorphic, be sure to take in extra calories throughout the day. Weight-gain powders and protein drinks complement your overall solid nutritional plan while boosting your caloric intake. Limit outside activities in order to save your energy for build-ing muscle mass.

TRAINING TIPS FOR THE ECTOMORPH

In a nutshell, the endomorph gains size quickly but has to fight to keep the fat off. The mesomorph, whom you will read about in the next chapter, is fit-ness's gifted body type, putting on lean muscle fairly easily with an average to below-average bodyfat level.

That leaves the ectomorph, who tends to be thin, lean, and lanky. Typi-cally, an ectomorph will have a short upper torso; long arms and legs; narrow chest, shoulders, feet, and hands; and long, thin muscles. Many ectomorphs who work out want more muscle size and weight. However hopeless it may seem for ectomorphs to gain size, they shouldn't give up. Many great athletes were at one time ectomorphs.

Here are some training and nutri-tion tips that are sure to help the ecto-morph in his or her desire to build muscle and gain strength.

IT'S TIME TO USE POWER MOVEMENTS AND TRAIN HEAVY

It's Also Time to Skip the Isolation Work

The ectomorph needs to lift heavy weights to hit the deep muscle fibers that will make the body grow. Don't waste your time on isolation or cable movements right now. If you're an ectomorph, you should do the follow-ing exercises regularly in your workouts:

For legs: squat, stiff-legged deadlift, donkey calf raise
For chest: dumbbell or barbell incline press
For back: chin-up; barbell, dumbbell, or T-bar row
For shoulders: dumbbell or barbell front press
For biceps: barbell or dumbbell curl
For triceps: close-grip bench press, dip, or lying EZ-bar French press

REST A LITTLE LONGER

Ectomorphs tend to train at a fast pace. But they would benefit greatly—both in recovery and strength—if they slowed down. Intense training is the stimulus that creates great workout results. Intensity can be accomplished in a number of ways; two of the best are lift-ing heavy and resting longer between sets, and training lighter with shorter rest times. Because high-intensity workouts are necessary to make the ectomorph grow, the focus should be on lifting heavier and taking longer rest periods between sets to ensure greater muscular recovery for maximum inten-sity and strength for each set.

Ectomorphs must also give their bodies adequate rest between workouts. The absolute *minimum* rest an ecto-morph needs is 48 hours between the same bodypart workouts. And ecto-morphs should never work a bodypart unless it has *fully* recovered from the previous workout. Because of their high metabolism, ectomorphs should get no less than seven and a half hours (prefer-ably eight to nine) of sleep every night.

DID SOMEONE SAY EAT?

Training is unquestionably an important element in the ectomorph's workout success, but good nutrition is too! In fact, one of the biggest reasons ectomorphs have so many problems is that they eat too many of the wrong foods, eat too little of the good foods, and don't eat often enough.

Let's simplify things. You should structure your diet in the following way:

1. Eat five to seven small meals daily.
2. Increase your daily protein intake to 1 to 1.5 grams of protein per pound of bodyweight.
3. Aim to raise protein intake to no less than 35 percent of your daily total caloric intake.
4. Have a protein shake 90 minutes *before* bedtime.
5. Carbs should be 45 percent of daily dietary intake.
6. Increase your intake of fibrous carbs (cauliflower, broccoli) while limiting your intake of simple sugars (fruits, honey).
7. Keep your fat intake to roughly 20 percent of your daily dietary intake.
8. Eat slower-burning glycemic index foods such as beans, sweet corn, lentils, yams, peas, nonfat dairy products, porridge, oats, and pasta.
9. Supplement with a good multivitamin/mineral.
10. Drink a lot of water throughout the day—at least 80 ounces.

HEY, JUST RELAX

Many ectomorphs are high-strung individuals. They're usually amped up and on the go. For such individuals, stress can be a problem because it affects your workout and training progress by producing cortisol, a catabolic (the opposite of anabolic) hormone.

Ectomorphs should practice slowing things down and relaxing. Try slowing your pace and take at least 10 minutes a day to be off alone and away from people and noise. In those 10 minutes, lie down or sit relaxed, close your eyes, inhale through your mouth and exhale through your nose, and slowly, softly repeat the words that make you relaxed and calm.

As you relax, feel your muscles relax and become heavy as if concrete weights were attached to them. Imagine that all stress is leaving your body and dissipating into the air. Nothing can bother you. You are in control.

SAVE YOUR ENERGY

Since many ectomorphs have metabolisms as fast as a greyhound's, their bodies tend to burn very quickly the food they eat. Many ectomorphs I've talked to complain they can't seem to get bigger or stronger. The reason is simple: they don't eat enough of the right foods, they don't train correctly, and they engage in too much activity.

If you're an ectomorph and your big goal is to pack on more size and strength, minimize all other activities outside of weight training. Your goal is to make sure your body uses all the consumed nutrients to recover and grow from your workouts.

If you must be involved in other physically demanding activities, be sure to take in extra calories—above those you already take in for working out—and get plenty of rest. Follow these guidelines and your weight- and strength-gaining problems will be history.

5

Training the Mesomorph

I think it's safe to say that meso-morphs achieve excellent results from working out. Putting on muscle is not a problem for the mesomorph, although it still takes effort, intensity, and perseverance. Mesomorphs, like endo- and ectomorphs, benefit from proper training and nutritional guide-lines. Here are a few:

- Using a combination of heavy power movements like squats, deadlifts, rows, and presses along with shaping movements such as laterals, pressdowns, dumbbell curls, and extensions can give the mesomorph better muscle qual-ity, proportion, and symmetry.
- Mesomorphs respond well to fairly long workouts (up to 80 minutes) and shorter rests between sets (no longer than 45 to 60 seconds). Staying within the 6- to 10-set and 6- to 12-rep range works well for the mesomorph.
- Working out four days a week, such as the two-on/one-off work-out, seems to give the meso-morph's body enough workout

frequency and stimulation for growth.

■ A balanced diet is generally good enough to help the mesomorph pack on size and strength. You don't need to overload your system with massive amounts of protein or carbs. Eat sensibly and keep the bodyfat to an acceptable level. Whatever your predominant body type, remember you are a combination of all three body types.

TRAINING TIPS FOR THE MESOMORPH

Fortunate are the mesomorphs. These genetically gifted people seem to get great training results by just thinking about it. Well, not quite that easily, but mesomorphs are among those who achieve great results quickly.

Yet, despite their propensity to achieve such results, mesomorphs need the right training and nutrition program to make the best gains possible.

SO WHAT'S A MESOMORPH?

The male mesomorph typically is muscular and naturally strong, with a long torso and a big, full chest. The female mesomorph is stronger, more muscular, and often more athletic than other women (or girls). A mesomorph's strength can increase very quickly, as can his or her muscular size, especially on the right program.

A mesomorph responds well to training that involves heavy, quick movements along with shaping exercises. The more varied the exercise program, the better the results. Take quads, for example. After a good warm-up, a mesomorph could begin with a great mass movement like squats, followed by hack squats or leg presses, finishing

with a shaping movement like leg extensions. For hamstrings, the mesomorph might begin with stiff-legged deadlifts, followed by a shaping movement such as standing leg curls. For calves, the first movement might be heavy standing calf raises followed by high-rep toe raises with light weight on the leg press.

THE MORE YOU CHANGE THINGS, THE BETTER

If you're a mesomorph, you should make repeated changes in the workout variables—that is, the number of sets, reps, and exercises; length of training sessions and rest; number of training days; amount of weight used; and various exercise angles. You should also vary your training intensity. A combination of three to four weeks of intense training followed by one to two weeks of lower-intensity training seems to promote growth and strength, and prevent training burnout.

THE FOOD FACTOR

Mesomorphs grow best when they get plenty of protein—at least one gram per pound of bodyweight daily—and keep their carb intake moderately high. The surprising thing about the majority of mesomorphs I know is that they can follow a diet with more than 20 percent of calories from fat (still far less than the typical American diet) and it actually helps them gain mass and strength! In fact, many mesomorphs can boost their strength levels simply by moderately increasing their fat and protein intake. Strange as it may sound, a tablespoon or two of peanut butter a day can do some amazing things for a mesomorph.

A mesomorph typically will make strength and muscle gains by keeping his or her bodyweight relatively steady and looking to only gradually increase muscle mass.

The days of bulking up by 20 or 30 pounds and then cutting down are over for the mesomorphs who want to gain the greatest amount of *quality* lean tissue. In fact, many believe that for all individuals, quality muscle size can be gained much more quickly when body-fat levels are held under about 18 percent for men and about 24 percent for women.

THE AEROBIC FACTOR

If strength and size are the goals, intense cardio work such as running should be kept to a minimum. Running long distances can be counterproductive. Many mesomorphs can lose lean muscle tissue quickly if they run over two miles three times weekly. Some mesomorphs have found wind sprints an excellent way to condition and build the hamstrings, quads, and calves, while aerobically conditioning the cardiovascular system.

If running isn't for you, try the stair stepper, stationary bike, racquet sports, jumping rope, hiking, or treadmill. Just make sure you don't overdo it. Three times per week, 25 to 30 minutes per session (5-minute warm-up, 15 to 20 minutes in your target heart range, 5-minute cool-down), will work well for burning fat.

Of course, you probably won't be able to do that when it comes to jumping rope. So jump for 3 to 12 minutes and rest only long enough to keep your heart range in the target zone. In fact, that's the key to all your cardiovascular exercise. To find your target heart range per minute, subtract your age from 220 and multiply by 0.6 and 0.8. That's where you should be exercising aerobically.

BE PATIENT AND STAY THE COURSE

Since the mesomorph can make outstanding gains quickly, some individuals might be inclined to push themselves to the limit. Intense training is great, but doing too much too quickly can lead to overtraining and injury.

Over the years, athletics has been rife with genetically gifted mesomorphs with the potential for phenomenal growth, strength, and speed. But overenthusiasm caused them to burn out, injure themselves, or lose motivation to continue training.

If you're a mesomorph, consider yourself fortunate. But be sensible with your training and nutrition. These two factors will help you reach your fitness and training potential. Stay committed to your training. Learn how your body type responds to various training methods, sets, and wraps. Structure your training to your body type's needs and you'll be successful.

PART II

The Workouts

6

Workout 1: The Classic Three-Day-Per-Week, Whole-Body Workout

Before we begin the first workout, let's take a moment to define a beginner: someone who would most likely begin with this workout. (However, many who have trained for years still swear by it.) A beginner is someone who has never lifted weights before, may have lifted years ago but stopped, or hasn't trained on a regular basis for over six months.

When does a beginner become an intermediate and move on to a new training program? One school of thought says that a beginner should use a combination of machines, cables, and freeweight exercises, including supersets and forced reps to get better workouts. Proponents of this system agree that a beginner is a beginner up until he or she can handle more weight; then he or she graduates to the intermediate level. I don't belong to this school of thought.

I believe, like many others, that a beginner should not rush through a beginner program. Developing a solid foundation by using basic exercises and excellent form will help ensure a lifetime of injury-free training. This is very important and should be the first and foremost goal for any serious beginner.

Many of today's top athletes once used this method as beginners and stayed on the system for almost a full year. Results speak for themselves. I know firsthand.

I followed this beginner's program for the first two years of my training and gained 65 pounds of muscle—drug-free! Moreover, after 20 years of training, I have not had a single injury. The same can happen for you. Building a solid foundation is the key.

I am amazed at what I see in the gyms today. I often see beginning trainees doing "finishing movements" when they don't even have much mass to finish or shape—like dumbbell concentration curls for 12-inch arms! I want to ask them, "Hey, what are you doing, shaping the bone?"

Some of the most common injuries among beginners result from doing too much too soon. As a beginner, one of the most difficult things you'll ever face is holding yourself back from adding those extra exercises, sets, reps, and plates before your body is ready for them.

Because beginners often make good gains very quickly, many fall into the trap of thinking more is better. This is true later in the training equation, but not at the novice stage. Let me tell you right now, stick with the basics that will build a rock-solid foundation and don't overtrain.

TRAIN BIG MUSCLES FIRST

Remember this rule of thumb: train your big muscle groups first. That means hitting legs, back, and chest before training delts and arms. Here's why.

Larger muscle groups demand more energy and more intensity to grow and get stronger than do smaller muscle groups. If you train the arms with all-out intensity and then do the chest immediately afterward, you won't have enough energy to generate the training intensity

When working out, the amount of time you spend isn't as important as what you do.

necessary to stimulate chest growth. Moreover, since the triceps are required in chest movements, your arms will fail more quickly than your pecs, which will hold back your chest training. Also, if you're not careful, the metabolic and neurologic demands from training a large muscle group can easily put your body into a state of overtraining, which can lead to decreased strength and energy as well as stalled gains.

That's why it's crucial that you get in the gym, work your body hard, and get out and rest! How long you spend in the gym is irrelevant; what counts is what you do when you're there. Always train your bigger muscles first, when your energy level is greatest.

HOW MUCH WEIGHT SHOULD YOU USE?

This is probably the most common question I am asked. Of course, I can't answer it for you, because everyone's level of strength is different. Take a little extra time to experiment and find the right weights for all the exercises you do. It won't take long, and it will be well worth whatever time you spend. Here's how you can do it.

Let's say you're doing an incline barbell press for the chest. With just the bar, press the weight up and down. Easy, isn't it? Now, take two 10-pound weights and place one on each end of the bar. Again, press the weight up and down, but this time do 10 reps. Was it easy? If it was really easy, add another 10-pounder (or "dime") on each side and do another 10 reps. If it wasn't so easy, try adding a 2½- or 5-pound plate on each side. Continue this process until it becomes tough to complete 8 to 10 reps. Once you can lift a weight for 10 reps, increase the weight by approximately 10 percent.

Of course, never sacrifice excellent form just for the sake of lifting heavier weights. The reality is, you need to overload your muscles with progressively heavier weight if you want them to grow and become stronger. But always keep in mind that in working out, weight is only a means to an end and never an end in itself. Making the muscle work hard with proper form is the name of the game.

BREATHING AND PROPER FORM

Most people breathe without thinking about it—that is, until they start working out. Proper workout form demands that you breathe correctly. Here's how to breathe for any exercise you do.

Take a deep breath before you start. When you reach the bottom position of each movement (which is most often where the most difficult portion of the movement begins), begin breathing out in a controlled manner until you reach the top position. Remember to inhale at the top or easiest part of the exercise, and exhale throughout the hardest part of the movement.

With proper form and a mind-to-muscle connection, your results could skyrocket.

THE IMPORTANCE OF NONTRAINING DAYS

Let's talk a little about days off. As a beginner, you're going to be brimming with enthusiasm for working out. After all, this is a new sport that promises to make your body look and feel great. But just as too little exercise won't stimulate your muscles to grow, too much won't either. It's much better for you to not do enough than to do too much.

Most beginners achieve growth, strength, and body-changing spurts unmatched by people who work out at advanced levels; their bodies seem to grow overnight. Many beginners are also resilient to overtraining. They can push themselves into what would normally be the overtraining zone, and their bodies adapt to those demands by growing and getting stronger very quickly.

If only it could last! But it doesn't. Soon the phenomenal growth rate slows down, and the beginning trainee enters the more-intensity-for-any-growth zone.

That's why you need to give your body plenty of rest—especially if it's still sore from the last workout—to keep it fresh and growing.

Never train a bodypart that's still sore from your last workout. By all means, stretch out and get blood flowing into the sore muscle area, but don't train that bodypart until it has fully recovered.

Follow your beginner program to the letter, and don't throw in an extra day of training just because you want your body to grow faster. It won't. If you're on a Monday–Wednesday–Friday program, take those remaining four days off for rest. And *take one complete week off from working out for every six to eight weeks of consistent training.*

MUSCLE SORENESS—A GOOD OR NOT SO GOOD THING?

If you're a beginner, one thing can be said with certainty: if you work out, you're going to get sore. Is soreness bad? Not necessarily. The majority of muscle soreness comes from microtears in the muscle fibers, the result of intense exercise. The body repairs these microtears very quickly.

Not only that, but the body also overcompensates during this recovery by making the muscles stronger, thus making it harder for microtearing to occur in the future. Hence, if you want to continue to grow and get stronger, you will have to progressively overload your muscles on a regular basis in future workouts. Progressive overload is the cornerstone of weight training success.

Muscle soreness can become a problem when the body is pushed too hard too fast. Use of high-intensity training principles like those used by more advanced bodybuilders—such as supersets, tri-sets, forced reps, drop sets, rest-pause, and negatives—can put the skids on a beginner's progress. The connective tissue and supporting skeletal

structures haven't yet strengthened sufficiently to sustain these kinds of workouts to get the full benefit and intended results that these intermediate and advanced principles offer.

Use muscle soreness as a gauge to measure workout intensity and effectiveness. Soreness can be a good thing if not taken to extremes. However, most pros will tell you that you don't need to get sore after every workout in order to grow and get stronger.

YOUR CHANGING NUTRITIONAL NEEDS

Most beginners are interested in one thing: quick results. Even if their training is right on target, if they neglect this one crucial component, they can kiss good-bye their dreams of changing their bodies. That component is diet.

So, how's your diet? It should include

- Four to six small meals per day
- 50 percent calories from carbs, 35 percent from protein, and 15 percent from fat
- A carb drink with 50 to 75 grams of carbs within 30 minutes after workout—a 12- to 16-ounce bottle or can of fruit juice works great.
- About 40 to 55 grams of protein within 90 minutes after working out

If you're missing any of these elements, then your diet is most likely holding you back from maximizing your workout success. All of these are sound nutritional strategies that will give you a head start on creating a great looking and feeling body while keeping bodyfat levels low.

WHAT SHOULD YOU EAT?

Let me give you a few recommendations. For protein, stick with lean sources, like beef (I recommend flank steak), skinless chicken and turkey, egg whites, and a whey- or egg-based protein powder. You have a number of choices when it comes to carbohydrates. For sustained energy, the complex carbs such as vegetables, rice, whole grains, and pasta work well. Simple carbs, including strawberries, melon, bananas, apples, and grapefruit, provide quick energy but should be eaten in moderation.

If eating four to six balanced meals each day is difficult, substitute a protein shake for one or two of your regular meals. These are ideal for anyone who has a busy schedule. I also strongly suggest you have a protein shake or protein meal about 90 minutes before bedtime. I found that as a hard-training beginning athlete, my body was in a near-constant state of hunger. I also discovered that the only thing that would keep my stomach from growling at night was a high-protein meal about 90 minutes or so before bedtime. Eating my final meal

Who has time to prepare six meals a day? Try drinking a nutritious shake for one or two of those meals.

at 6 or 7 P.M., and then waiting a full twelve hours before breakfast, left me feeling weak, flat, and lethargic. The extra late-night protein meal was the perfect answer. Make sure, however, that you don't eat too close to bedtime.

WHEN TO CHANGE YOUR WORKOUT

Often, a new trainee will find a routine and stick with it, not because it works (though it may have been a great one at one time), but because it's comfortable, and change requires thought. Changing your routine, however, not only signifies a jump to a higher level (for example, from beginner to intermediate), but also stimulates your muscles in new, growth-creating ways. When to change your training cannot be generalized: genetics, training goals, previous experience, desire, existing level of strength and growth development are all major factors that must be considered before you move to the next level.

As a rule, stay on your beginner program for at least four months. Training longer at this level certainly will not hurt you. During these four months, you should develop excellent exercise form, find your body's own exercise groove using the basic movements, strengthen your muscles and connective tissue, and establish the all-important mind-muscle link for increased intensity and greater results.

Once you become an intermediate, you'll notice a number of changes: you're working out more frequently with more sets and heavier weights, using high-intensity training principles, increasing nutrient uptake and supplementation, and needing more rest.

Most likely, you will want to add a few shaping movements to your routine. For someone wanting to gain muscle size, the emphasis on his or her training should be 90 percent compound movements and 10 percent isolation-shaping movements. Remember, you've got to have the size before you start chiseling your body!

BUILDING THE FOUNDATION

The greatest athletic bodies of men and women of yesterday and today were developed through basic exercises. Here's a list of some of the best:

- Chest—bench press, incline press, dip, flye
- Back—chin-up, deadlift, T-bar row, one-arm dumbbell row, bent-over row, seated row, pulldown
- Quads—squat, hack squat, leg press
- Hamstrings—stiff-legged deadlift, leg curl
- Calves—donkey, standing, and seated calf raise

- Shoulders—barbell and dumbbell overhead press, dumbbell side lateral raise
- Traps—shrug, upright row
- Biceps—standing barbell curl, alternate dumbbell curl
- Triceps—dip, close-grip bench press, overhead or lying French press, pressdown
- Abdominals—reverse crunch, crunch

THE BEGINNER'S WORKOUT

One of the best beginner programs is the three-days-a-week routine. For example, do a whole-body workout on Monday, Wednesday, and Friday. The other days are for rest. Begin your workout with your legs, your biggest muscle group. Here's the routine:

Exercise	Sets	Reps
Legs		
Leg extension (warm-up)	2	15
Squat	2	8
Leg curl	2	10
Standing calf raise	2	10–15

Leg extension

Squat

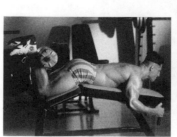
Leg curl

Standing calf raise

Exercise	Sets	Reps
Chest (needs warm-up)		
Incline barbell bench press	2	8
Flat bench dumbbell flye	2	8–10
Back		
Chin-up *or*	2	8–10
pulldown	2	10–15
Bent-over row	2	6–10
Shoulders		
Seated overhead press		
(barbell or dumbbell)	2	8–10
Upright row	2	10–15

Incline barbell bench press

Flat bench dumbbell flye

Chin-up

Bent-over row

Pulldown

Seated overhead press (a)

Seated overhead press (b)

Upright row (a)

Upright row (b)

Exercise	Sets	Reps
Biceps		
Standing barbell curl	2	5–9
Triceps		
Dip *or*	2	limit
pressdown	2	10–15
Abdominals		
Crunch	2	20–30

Standing barbell curl

Dip

Pressdown

Crunch

7

Workout 2:
The Four-On/One-Off Workout

Here's a little piece of advice you should always remember: *it's not how long you train that matters; it's what you do when you train.* For example, your best buddy might work out for two hours, but with average intensity. Yet, if you work out for only 30 minutes but with much higher intensity, you'll get far better results. Intensity makes the difference.

Think of intensity as how hard and effectively you can make a muscle work during a given period. Obviously, if your chest workout calls for 12 sets and you've just finished your second, do you really think you'll be able to train with all-out intensity for the next 10 sets? Don't kid yourself. If, however, you've just done your second set for chest and you've only got 3 more sets to do, you'll probably be able to give those remaining sets all you've got. When the sheer number of sets becomes your primary workout goal, you miss the whole point of strength training, which is to work the muscle with higher levels of intensity for higher levels of results.

TIME FOR THE NEXT LEVEL

Using the beginner program, you trained the whole body three times per week. Now it's time to get into split training, where you'll work out four days per week, but train the entire body only twice.

This workout is a four-day split, and it's one of the best training programs around. You'll work your upper body one day, work your legs the next, rest a day, hit the upper body again on the fourth day, work your legs again on the fifth day, and then take two complete days off from training. The four-day split allows you to do more exercises, handle more weight, and train each bodypart more intensely. It also gives your body adequate time to recuperate, which means better results.

WHAT KIND OF RESULTS CAN YOU EXPECT?

First of all, you can expect to increase your size and strength. You will do more exercises and sets, handle more weight, and execute some specialization work for those weak bodyparts. Your body will start to become a high-performance machine. Your body will handle a lot more intensive work, and in the process, it will adapt to those demands wonderfully. You will get more out of your body than ever before. Not only that, you will also blast through self-imposed preconceptions about just how good your body can look and feel.

THE EXERCISES

As you recall, the three-day-a-week program emphasized the use of basic exercises performed with barbells and dumbbells. The four-day program will keep these core exercises, but also add cables and machines. Muscles respond well when you work them from a variety of angles, which means using whatever modality of training is at your disposal.

THE FOUR-DAY SPLIT PROGRAM

Monday and Thursday–Upper Body

Exercise	Sets	Reps
Chest		
Barbell incline press	3	6–8
Dumbbell press	3	8–10
Incline, decline, or flat bench flye	2	10–12
Back		
Chin-up *or*	3	limit
machine pulldown	3	12–15
Dumbbell row	2	8
Seated cable row	2	8–10
Deadlift (only once per week)	3	6

Incline bench flye

Dumbbell row

Seated cable row

Deadlift

Exercise	Sets	Reps
Shoulders		
Seated dumbbell press	3	8–10
Dumbbell side lateral	3	10–14
Barbell shrug	2	5–8
Biceps		
Seated dumbbell incline curl	3	6–9
EZ-bar preacher curl	3	10–15
Triceps		
Pressdown	4	12–18
Lying EZ-bar extension	3	8–10
Abs		
Hanging knee raise	3	limit
Crunch	3	8–10

Dumbbell side lateral raise

Barbell shrug

Seated dumbbell incline curl

EZ-bar preacher curl

Pressdown

Lying EZ-bar extension

Hanging knee raise

Tuesday and Friday—Lower Body

Exercise	Sets	Reps
Legs		
Leg extension (warm-up)	2	15–20
Front squat	4	8–10
Leg press (feet wide, toes pointed out)	3	10–20
Leg curl	4	12–20
Standing leg curl	3	10–15
Standing calf raise	4	8–20
Seated calf raise	3	8–12

Wednesday, Saturday, and Sunday

Off

Front squat

Leg press

Leg curl

Seated calf raise

USE THE BEST FORM FOR THE BEST RESULTS

If you want size and strength, then continually strive to lift heavier poundages whenever possible. But keep in mind that to make a muscle grow, you must work it with intensity. Proper form is a major prerequisite for muscle growth and workout success. You can use terrible form and still intensely work and overload a muscle; however, you do so at great risk of injury. Feel every rep. If the weight you're using doesn't allow you to feel every rep, by all means reduce it. The majority of people working out would do well to remember that *weight is only a means to an end and never an end in itself.*

HOW MUCH WEIGHT SHOULD YOU USE?

After being on the three-day program, you should have a good idea of how much weight you can handle for the basic movements. While I strongly believe that you should warm up thoroughly before lifting heavy, I also believe that you shouldn't waste valuable time and energy once you're warmed up.

For example, let's say you're doing dumbbell presses and your best is using 60-pound dumbbells for 6 to 8 reps. On your first 2 warm-up sets, do 30 pounds for 10 reps. Then on your first heavy set, go right to the 60-pound dumbbells and crank out 6 to 8 or more reps. On your second heavy set, reduce the weight by 10 percent and crank out another 6 to 8 reps. On the third set, reduce the weight by another 10 percent and bang out another 6 to 8 reps. Then you're finished with that movement.

WHAT ABOUT FOOD?

Your four-day workout diet should remain very similar to the three-days-per-week diet outlined earlier in the book: high complex carbs, moderate protein, and low fat. However, because you're adding an extra day of training and increasing workout intensity, you'll raise the carbs and protein a bit.

First of all, to restore depleted muscle fuel (glycogen) used during your workout, always have a carb drink (at least 30 to 70 grams) within 30 minutes after your workout. This 30-minute time period after the workout can be extremely important for refueling muscle and liver glycogen.

About 40 minutes after you have the carb drink, have a good protein meal. If that's not possible, then be sure to have a good meal of carbs and protein within 90 minutes after your workout. Of course, keep your water intake high throughout the day—at least 80 ounces, and more if possible.

I'll tell you a trick that has helped me keep my waist size down while I put on size and strength. In the meal immediately following my workout and on the days my body was sore, I doubled my protein intake—sometimes tripled it! After the soreness reached its peak and began to diminish, I slowly reduced my protein intake until it was back down to normal maintenance levels. My carb and fat intake remained consistent. Using this trick gave my body the extra protein it needed when it needed it. And my body recovered much more

quickly from the hard workouts. Try it and watch what happens.

BE CALM AND COOL

Be prepared: the four-day split program will tax your recuperative capacities more than the three-day beginner program. That's why I suggest that you get in the gym, work out very intensely, and then get the heck out!

Another thing I strongly advise is not to train too late at night. Training too close to bedtime can keep you awake and prevent you from getting the needed seven to nine hours of sleep each night.

And a word about getting frustrated with your workouts . . . don't! If today's workout didn't allow you to lift any heavier, do more reps, or get a better pump, it's no big deal. In the grand scheme of things, as it relates to your body and fitness, it won't make any difference. Be kind to yourself and tell yourself that with the next workout you'll do better. End of story. Now rest and enjoy!

ALWAYS CHANGE YOUR WORKOUTS

I want you to always change your workouts. Each workout, use different exercise combinations, reps, weights, angles, and rest periods. Any or all of the warning signs that follow might indicate that it is time to change your workouts:

- No increases in weights used
- Little, if any, muscle or strength gains
- Boredom
- You've been on the same program for six weeks or more

This four-day workout is meant solely as a guide. Use it and keep only those exercises that work for you and throw away the rest. Experiment and find other exercises that give you great results, and use them regularly. However, always change the order and other workout variables to keep your body off-guard. The bottom line is keep your workouts fresh and exciting.

HOW TO KNOW WHEN TO MOVE TO THE NEXT LEVEL

If you're progressing from three days a week to the four-day program, *stay on the four-day workout for at least five months.* Remember, this four-day split is so good that many athletes who have been training for years still use it. You cannot beat barbell and dumbbell exercises, period!

The kind of exercises you do aren't as important as you may think. Sure, they're necessary to work the muscles. However, *how effectively you make that exercise work a particular bodypart is what determines the results.* The sooner you give up on looking for a magical exercise to change a bodypart, the sooner you'll start using your own mind and finding your own creative ways to make any exercise work for you!

8

Intensity Tips You Can Use

SIMPLE WAYS TO MAKE YOUR WORKOUTS BETTER

I've talked a lot about intensity. Are you catching the drift as to just how important it is to your workout success? Good. I'm going to give you some excellent intensity principles that will kick your workouts and body into some serious results.

- Superset—In this technique you group two exercises together for opposing muscle groups, such as biceps curls and triceps pressdowns. Remember, as soon as you finish the set of biceps curls, immediately do a set of triceps pressdowns.

- Pyramid—This process has you increase the weight you use with each set. For example, begin your first set with 60 percent of your one-rep max weight and increase the weight by 10 percent each succeeding set. You can also do the opposite: warm up for a few sets, use your heaviest weight for 6 to 8 reps, and then decrease the weight by 10 percent each succeeding set.

- Compound set—In this technique you perform two back-to-back exercises for the same bodypart with little or no rest—such as doing barbell curls immediately followed by a set of seated dumbbell incline curls.

- Cycle training—Despite what some advocates of all-time high-intensity training might say, real-world experience shows that many people who train heavy all the time are at greater risk of injury than those who cycle their training. The body is not a machine and can't be continually pushed and endlessly pounded without periods of rest and cycled training. There are three cycles you might want to use at various times in your training:

1. Mass cycle—moderate to heavy weights, no more than 90 seconds of rest between sets; 6 to 10 reps for upper body and 8 to 20 reps for lower body
2. Power cycle—heavy weights and 3 to 8 reps for lower- and upper-

body movements with up to three minutes rest between sets

3. Cut cycle—light to moderate weights, 12 to 25 reps, and no more than 45 seconds of rest between sets

Many people get great results by staying on each cycle for six to eight weeks and then taking one full week off from training before moving to the next cycle.

■ Isotension—Feeling a muscle work is the key to getting the most from any exercise. To help create this mind-muscle link, regularly practice isotension. Without using any weights, you flex the muscle you've been working and hold it in the peak contracted position for three to six seconds. Do this three times at the end of the last set of every bodypart workout.

From big muscles to small muscles, intensity is the secret to great results.

■ Muscle confusion—Your body adapts very quickly to the physical demands you place upon it. If you do the same routine in the same way over and over, your body will stop responding. That's why you need to change your workouts, exercises, sets, reps, weights, rest periods, angles, and degrees of intensity every time you work out. By doing so, you will keep your body off-guard, and you'll continue to grow and get stronger.

TIME TO DO LESS TO GET BETTER RESULTS

A strange workout phenomenon occurs after you've been training for about six months: your rate of results slows down. When you began training, your body responded, grew, and seemed to change overnight. That was exciting. Yet, after you have continued to train, your body still responds, but not nearly as fast. In fact, you probably have had to work more to get less. That's no fun.

But they say patience is a virtue, and this is never truer than in working out. Many people quit when those incredibly fast results start to slow down. Many people I've talked to had their strength, muscle mass, and workout gains slow down the most after three years of conventional sets-and-reps training. However, when the same people reduced the number of sets, exercises, and training days, and increased the rest time between workouts, their great workout results continued to go up steadily—regardless of how many years they had been training.

What these successful people discovered was that as their bodies became stronger, their ability to generate higher levels of workout intensity increased. In other words, it took less time to produce better workouts. Instead of taking 12 sets to fatigue the chest, they could do it with 6 or less! In fact, many could easily do it with just 1 or 2 sets.

Doing less accomplishes two things. First, less workout time is needed to produce better results. Second, any effort beyond what is required to stimulate growth and strength is considered overtraining. For the smart trainee, it all comes down to experimentation. For some, if 6 sets can stimulate growth, what about 4? If 4 sets can do it, how about 3 all-out sets? Find the right number for you. A book or magazine won't tell you—your body will!

YOU NEED TO KNOW HOW IMPORTANT IT IS TO TAKE FORCED REST BREAKS

So if you, as an advanced trainee, can now generate greater power and intensity much more quickly, then your workouts should be better and take less time. The question is, what do you do with all that "free time" away from the gym? Rest and enjoy your life!

The greater physiological demands in training intensity require that you give your body more rest. Hard workouts zap your central nervous system as well as your muscles and connective tissue. One world-record-strength athlete told me that his body needs 21 days—three full weeks—to recover after an all-out lift. And look at how many people freak out if they miss two or three days of training!

I know some advanced workout folks who think they're ready to work the same bodypart just two days following a tough workout. They live by the erroneous belief that they'll lose strength and get small or flabby if they don't regularly train hard. Not so. The truth is, they'll get small and lose strength *because they haven't allowed enough time for recovery!*

Do not wait until you stop getting great workout results or have an injury before taking a layoff. *Take an extra day off from training any time your body is still sore from a previous workout. And take a complete week off from training every six to eight weeks.* If you think you'll get weak or out of shape, you won't. Remember, you are the one that controls your body. Your body doesn't control you unless you give it that power!

9

Workout 3: The One-On/One-Off, Two-On/Two-Off Workout

I could write a whole book of nothing but advanced workouts, but that wouldn't help you find the workouts best suited for your body type, genetics, goals, and level of commitment. Here's one I think you'll like.

THE ONE-ON/ONE-OFF, TWO-ON/TWO-OFF WORKOUT

All Training Days

Stationary bike (5-minute general warm-up)

Stretching (10 minutes)

Day One

Exercise	Sets	Reps
Quads		
Front squat (shoulder-width stance, feet pointed slightly outward)	3	6–10
Leg press (feet wide and pointed out)	3	8–12
Sissy squat	2	to failure
Hamstrings		
Lying leg curl	3	10–20
Stiff-legged deadlift	3	6–8

NOTE: For the stiff-legged deadlift, use dumbbells one workout and a barbell the next. Pyramid the weight, making your last set the heaviest.

Quad stretch

Chest stretch

Sissy squat

Exercise	Sets	Reps
Calves		
Tri-set the following exercises in this order:*		
Standing calf raise (heavy)	3	5–8
Donkey calf raise (moderate)	3	9–12
Seated calf raise (light)	3	12–20

NOTE: You must go nonstop from one machine to another. Rest no longer than 45 seconds between tri-sets.

Day 2

Rest

Donkey calf raise

Day 3

Exercise	Sets	Reps
Chest		
Incline dumbbell press	4	6–8
Flat bench dumbbell press		
(compound set with)	3	8–10
Close-hand push-up	3	to failure
Back		
Chin-up (wide-grip)		
(compound set with)	4	to failure
T-bar row (wide or close-grip)	4	8
Seated cable row	3	8–12

Close-hand push-up

T-bar row

Day 4

Exercise	Sets	Reps
Delts		
Bent-over dumbbell lateral raise	4	12–16
Seated barbell press (wide-grip)		
(compound set with)	3	12
Standing dumbbell side		
lateral raise	3	20

NOTE: Use light weights with very strict nonstop reps.

Traps		
Shrug (alternate barbells and		
dumbbells each workout with)	3	5–8
Cable upright row (use a		
close-grip with straight bar)	2	12–20
Triceps		
Lying EZ-bar French press		
(compound set with)	4	8–10
Pressdown (straight bar)	4	16–20

Bent-over dumbbell lateral raise

Shrug

Exercise	Sets	Reps
Biceps		
Standing barbell curl (do drop sets, working from heavy to light)	5	15, 12, 10, 8, 6
Seated *or* lying dumbbell curl (lie on your back with upper arms at a 45-degree angle away from bench)	3	10–15

Seated dumbbell incline curl

Day 5

Off

Day 6

Off

HOW TO TURN THIS INTO A THREE-ON/ONE-OFF, THREE-ON/TWO-OFF WORKOUT

Simply do two bodyparts, instead of three, each workout and add an extra day to work those bodyparts. For example:

Day 1—chest, back
Day 2—legs, hamstrings, calves
Day 3—shoulders, triceps, and biceps
Day 4—rest
Day 5—repeat day 1
Day 6—repeat day 2
Day 7—repeat day 3
Day 8—rest

Every other week, add an extra day of rest so the workout will look like the following. You choose whatever bodyparts you want to work each day.

Day 1—work out
Day 2—work out
Day 3—work out
Day 4—rest
Day 5—rest
Day 6—begin new workout cycle

Regardless of which workout you do, always change things around. Don't always do chest and back together. One workout do chest and triceps, the next workout do biceps and back, and the third workout do legs and delts. Keep it fresh and new, always change the order around, and definitely change the exercises, sets, reps, weights, rest, angles, and anything else you can think of. This will help you find the best routines that work for you.

KEEP USING THE ROUTINES THAT WORK BEST FOR YOU

Remember that workout logbook I told you about? Well, the more advanced you become, the more you'll find yourself returning to your logbook for routines that worked. In fact, you'll find that alternating beginning and intermediate workouts with your advanced training will produce excellent gains.

Forget about training incredibly hard all the time. For great long-term results—without the wear and tear on the body—you simply don't need to do that. Cycling your workouts with excellent beginner, intermediate, and advanced routines will pay the greatest workout rewards.

10

More Tips for Great Results

WEAK-POINT TRAINING

Every 10 weeks, pick a bodypart that you would like to improve. Train that bodypart—and no other—every day for seven days. At the end of the seven days, take five days off from working that bodypart. After the rest period, resume training the bodypart using your regular routines.

    This will allow one week of specific-bodypart-only training for each of the five major muscle groups (chest, back, legs, shoulders, and arms) in a one-year period. A great way to jump-start some serious gains!

WEAK-LINK TRAINING

Want to blast out of the training rut? Do weak-link training. Specifically, train the weakest point in any given exercise. For example, let's say your squat poundage won't go up. What can you do? Two things: first, use a power rack, adjust the rack pins, and do sets of quarter- and half-range movements. Second, without using

the power rack, do a regular squat, but stop each rep at the bottom position for two seconds, then come back up and repeat. These dead stops will give you incredible power from the bottom position. You can also do power-rack and dead-stop training on presses and deadlifts with equally great results. I suggest doing dead-stop and power-rack training once every two weeks.

SINGLE-EXERCISE, HEAVY-BASIC MOVEMENTS

A good beginner program will allow you to make consistent, excellent gains. As an advanced trainee, going back to single-exercise, heavy-basic movements will work wonders after you've been doing workout after workout of multiple exercises, isolation movements, cables, and so on.

Simply pick one basic movement for each bodypart. Use only that exercise on the day you train that bodypart. Do 6 sets of 6 reps, but go heavy. Do this every sixth workout and watch what happens!

FLUCTUATING REPS

You know by now that if you constantly shock the body with new exercises, sets, reps, weights, rest periods, and angle combinations, you will grow. No two ways about it.

A great way to great results is by playing around with different rep variables in your workouts. One workout, go heavy and do triples (3-rep sets). Next workout, go light and do high reps with minimal rest between sets. *Always change the variables in your training.* Never, ever, do the same thing twice.

11

Workout 4: The 10 System, Part I

Many of the people you see working out are an amazing bunch. They know what it takes to build muscle, gain strength, and change their bodies; yet, like so many others, they continue to look for that magic pill, powder, and exercise that will make all the difference in the world. Sorry to disappoint you, but such a thing simply doesn't exist—it never has. When it comes to great workout results—building muscle, size, and power—things haven't changed much in the last 40 years.

You still have to go to the gym (or lift at home); you must work out intensely (don't confuse working out intensely with how much time you spend working out); you must eat good wholesome nutritious foods with plenty (about 45 percent) of lean protein (fish, chicken, turkey, egg whites, tofu, protein powder, and nonfat dairy products like yogurt, cottage cheese, and skim milk), a moderate amount (about 35 percent) of complex carbs (vegetables, grains, beans, and legumes), some simple carbs (fruits like melons, strawberries, apples, and some bananas), and keep your fat

content fairly low, roughly 15 percent to 20 percent of your total dietary intake. Having done all that, you need to get plenty of rest—about seven to nine hours of sleep each night—and keep your stress levels as low as possible. This is especially important today, because we live in a stress-filled world and our lives are incredibly busy. Each day, even if it's for only 5 to 10 minutes, you must find a place to be alone and relax.

So, you say that you can do all that without a problem. Yet your training needs a major boost, something different to get your mind motivated and your body growing and getting great results again. What can you do? Actually, you can do a lot. But to tell you exactly what *you* need to do right now would require me to see your physique and ask you many questions about your training, nutrition, mental approach, goals, desires, and much more.

Instead, I'm going to give you a series of workouts that you will probably find to be quite different from what you've been used to seeing in books and other magazines. I call them microsystems because they target specific areas of the body unlike other training methods. These new ways to train borrow the best ideas—along with many new ones—from the tried-and-true training systems that have brought great results to people all over the world.

Only a handful of real training systems are out there (e.g., Heavy Duty, PHA, Power Factor, Static Contraction). Many of the routines you see and read about simply consist of smatterings of many different systems. Rarely do you find someone who trains purely on one given system for months or years at a time. Neither should you. Your body thrives and needs change, and it needs it every single time you work out. *Every time you work out, do something different.*

That's how you keep your body off-guard, growing, and getting stronger.

This microsystem should only be used for one week per every 8 to 10 weeks you train. That is, you will do this and only this microsystem during that one week. But you won't do it every day of that week. You'll only do this routine three times during that one week. Here's how it will work.

You will focus on hitting the deepest fibers in your biggest muscles. You will stay away from machines, as much as you can, and isolation exercises during this one week. Your focus will be on building more size and strength in and on your body. And you will use the 10 System to do it.

For some strange reason, most people get great results from using 10 reps. Of course, this general observation is by no means carved in stone. Nevertheless, it is a good starting point for us. Although I'll be the first to tell you to always train each muscle with the highest intensity you can—whether using heavy weight and low reps, lighter weight and high reps, moderate weight, low to high reps and minimal rest, or anything in between—*for this one week, I want you to do three exercises of 10 sets of 10 reps for only three muscle groups. That's one exercise per muscle group.*

QUADS

Let's take legs. For this one week, I want you to forget about hamstrings and calves. You can concentrate on them during the next eight to ten weeks. All I want you to work on now is the major leg muscle: the quads.

Squats

The king of all quad exercises, and arguably the best single-weight resistance exercise, is the squat. Front or back squats, take your pick. Next on the list are either leg presses or hack squats. These are the only three leg exercises that I want you to pick from. Just for this one week I really want you to push yourself, so go ahead and pick the toughest leg exercise you can do. Once you've chosen the exercise, I want you to begin with it (of course, after a good warm-up) and do *10 sets of 10 reps.*

After 1 or 2 warm-up sets (which do not count), go up to a weight you know you can do for a few sets of 10 reps and stay there. Don't change weights between sets. At this weight, you should be breathing and pushing fairly hard once you reach the seventh or eighth rep. Do not rest any longer than 90 seconds between sets.

If you're doing back squats, keep the bar high on the traps, set your feet at about shoulder width and pointed straight ahead, and lower the weight until your thighs are *at least* parallel with the floor. Keep your back fully upright and your head looking up and straight ahead. Take a deep breath as you go down and give a big exhale as soon as you start coming up.

Keep the reps going, and as much as you will want to, *don't stop between reps.* Keep the quads burning, and let the incredible intensity you will generate turn on those deep muscle fibers.

LATS

Chin-Ups

The next exercise you will do for 10 sets of 10 reps will be chin-ups using a wider-than-shoulder-width grip. Get a spotter to hold your legs or waist if you can't do 10 reps. And strap an extra 20 to 40 pounds around your waist if you can easily do 10 reps. If there is no way you can do 10 sets of 10 reps on the

When doing squats, you want your thighs to come parallel with the floor.

Machines are great, but there's nothing like a chin-up with just your bodyweight.

chin-up and you can't find a spotter, then do reverse-grip pulldowns, but with a heavy weight. I'll describe how to do both.

First, the chin-ups. With your hands set wider than your shoulders, take an overhand grip on the bar. Allow your body to completely hang down with your arms locked out. Now, *pull yourself up until your nose is even with the bar.* Slowly lower yourself back down until your arms are locked out again. No half reps, fast reps, or cheating. When you start getting tired and feel yourself jerking or twisting your body just to get your nose up to the bar level, get a spotter. Have that spotter hold the back of your legs or shoes, which will be behind you because your legs will be bent. The spotter should only give you enough help so you will barely make it to nose level on the bar each rep. I want you to really push yourself on this and not cheat. *Rest only 60 seconds between sets and don't rest between reps.*

If you're doing the reverse-grip pulldown, grab an overhead pulldown bar with your palms up, and keep your hands about six to eight inches apart. While keeping your upper body fully erect with just a slight lean backward, bring the bar down and pull your elbows straight back behind you as far as you can, until you've fully contracted your back muscles. Slowly allow the bar to come up and do the next rep.

After you've done 10 sets of 10 reps of either the chin-ups or pulldowns, stretch your back and lats by taking a grip on a stationary bar with your palm facing away from your body. If you grip the bar with your right hand, your right palm will face the bar and point away from your body. Keep your arm straight and at least at shoulder height. Count for 30 seconds, then do the other side. You can also stretch

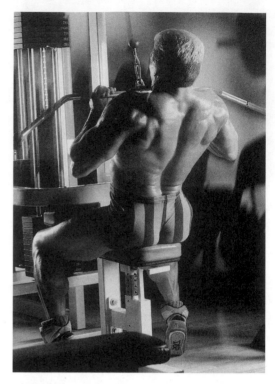

Reverse-grip pulldowns are great for working your back.

your lats by hanging from a chinning bar. After that, you're ready for the last exercise: the shoulder press.

DELTS

Many people, especially the guys who want to become wider and get that V-taper, ask how they can do it if they weren't born with a wide bone structure. I say do exercises that specifically target the deepest muscles of the shoulders. And you would be hard-pressed to find a better exercise for this than shoulder presses.

Shoulder Press

I will let you decide which shoulder press to use, barbell or dumbbell. Whichever one you choose, always be sure to warm up first. Take a few light sets of using a light weight, just the bar, or a few light weights on each side until your delts are warmed up. Then, just like squats, go up to a weight you can do for a few sets of 10 reps, but that will also get you breathing fairly heavy and pushing pretty hard after about the seventh or eighth rep. If you're using the barbell, take a slightly wider-than-shoulder-width grip and lower the bar to either in front of you, where you will lower it below your chin, or behind you, where you will lower it to your upper traps.

Like the other two exercises, *don't stop between reps and don't rest longer than 50 seconds between sets.* I want you to keep the delts burning, and doing 10 sets of 10 reps will give you a burn like you've never had before!

After you've done 10 sets of 10 reps on the shoulder press, you are finished—physically and mentally. Great job! The only thing I want you to do now is go to the locker room, grab your stuff, and get the heck out of the gym and eat something. *Right after this workout, drink a can of fruit juice* so you can refill that muscle glycogen supply as quickly as possible. Then, within 40 to 90 minutes, eat a good meal with a lot of protein and a moderate amount of carbohydrates. Give your body 48 hours of rest, and then you'll do the same three exercises, 10 sets of 10 reps for each exercise.

During this one week of 10 sets of 10 reps, you will either work out on Monday–Wednesday–Friday or Tuesday–Thursday–Saturday. All the other days you will not do any cardio or any other kind of training. All I want you to do is rest!

Don't be too worried about not working your chest, calves, hamstrings, arms, and abs. Doing 10 sets of 10 reps, with these key major muscle exercises, will work many more muscles than you may think. And you'll work your body in ways that will make it explode with new growth and strength, without overtraining.

Most important, keep your mind focused and the picture burning brightly of how you want your body to look and feel. The mental training is just as important, if not more, than your actual workout. Where the mind goes, the body follows!

To really work your delts, keep the weight moving and don't rest between sets.

12

Workout 5: The 10 System, Part II

So are you becoming gigantic and unbelievably strong yet? If you've been using the 10 System, training hard, eating the right foods in the right quantities and at the right times, and getting enough rest, then you should be growing like a weed.

In the last chapter, I gave you the first three exercises to do when using the 10 System: squats, chin-ups, and shoulder presses. You should use the 10 System for only one week per every eight to ten weeks of training. During this one week, you only do these three exercises—and no others. You will do 10 sets of 10 reps for each exercise three times during that one week with a complete day of rest between workouts (for example, Monday–Wednesday–Friday).

You can use the 10 System all year round; however, each time you use it (one week for every 8 to 10 weeks of training), use different exercises and work different bodyparts. Here's the first workout to show what I mean.

- 8 to 10 weeks of regular training
- Then one week of three workouts using three exercises of 10 sets of 10 reps

- First 10 System workout will be squats, chin-ups, and shoulder presses

This is what your first 8 to 10 weeks of regular training and first workout using the 10 System would be. Now, after the next 8 to 10 weeks of regular training, do the following 10 System second workout.

CHEST

30-Degree Incline Dumbbell Press—10 sets of 10 reps

I believe this is one of the most, if not the most, effective chest building and strengthening exercises you can do. The degree of stretch and movement is incredible, if you do it right.

You need to first warm up, but before you do that, set the incline bench to a roughly 30-degree angle. Why 30 degrees? Because this angle allows your chest work to concentrate more on the pecs rather than on the deltoids, which happens when the bench is raised higher, such as 45

Use a 30-degree incline for your incline chest work.

degrees. I suggest doing one or two light sets of 8 to 10 reps to get the blood pumping and the delts, pecs, and triceps warmed. After your warm-up, go right up to a weight that you can do with moderate effort for 7 to 8 reps and that you can do for 10 reps if you push yourself on the eighth, ninth, or tenth rep. Stay at this weight until you've done 10 sets of 10 reps. You should rest no longer than 60 seconds between sets, and keep the reps moving during each set without resting between reps.

Keep your glutes tight against the seat and your back firmly against the backpad. Be sure to bring your elbows straight down toward the floor and not back behind you, and bring the dumbbells down until the dumbbell weight plates are even with your chest. You must lower the weights down as far as possible in order to get a good stretch. As you bring the weights back up and over you, be sure not to allow the weights to touch each other. At the top

of the movement, keep the weights about six to eight inches apart. After you've done 10 sets of 10 reps, you're ready to move to the next exercise: stiff-legged deadlifts.

HAMSTRINGS

Stiff-Legged Barbell or Dumbbell Deadlift

Leg curls are not a bad exercise, if it's the only one you can do. But if you want the killer of all hamstring movements, you can't do much better than stiff-legged deadlifts. Not only do they work the hamstrings, but they also work the traps, shoulders, forearms, and muscles in the lower back like the erectors. But you must do them in a certain way to get the best results possible.

Using as close to perfect form as possible is a must, not only to prevent

The key to a great hamstring workout is a full stretch and a powerful contraction.

injury, but to isolate the hamstrings and hit those deep muscle fibers. Here's how to do them.

- Stand on a wooden platform elevated at least four inches or a flat bench.
- Take a shoulder-width grip on a barbell. You can use an overhand grip or a combination grip of one hand over and one hand under.
- Holding the weight with your arms locked out and your body fully erect, bend your upper torso over until the bar is lowered as far down as possible.
- Some people will be able to lower the bar until it touches the top of their feet. Others may only be able to bring the barbell down to shin level.
- Bend your knees, but only slightly. You want to make sure your hamstrings are fully stretched.
- Do not round your back as you lower the weight. Keep your back flexed and tight, as this is not a lat movement.
- While keeping your arms locked out during the entire movement, bring your upper torso back up to the fully upright and erect position.
- Always use a controlled movement throughout the whole rep. Never bounce or jerk your body or the weight.
- Keep the barbell close to your body from start to finish.
- Do 10 sets of 10 reps.
- Rest no longer than 45 seconds between sets and do not rest between reps.

For variety, or if you can't do or don't have barbells, do the next best thing: stiff-legged dumbbell deadlifts. You'll basically do these much the same way as I described for the barbell; however, the big differences will be in how you hold the dumbbells and your arm and hand positions when you bend over.

At the top of the movement, keep your upper body erect and the dumbbells to your sides. As you bend over, bring your arms around to the front of you until the dumbbells and your palms face your shins.

BICEPS

Seated Palms-Up Dumbbell Curl, Three-Fourths Range of Movement

You'll do this last exercise for the big arms. Go ahead and admit it, it's hard to beat a pair of great looking arms. This exercise will really work your biceps if you do it exactly as follows.

- Use a flat bench or a miniseat with a small backpad that you would use for doing shoulder presses.
- After a good warm-up of one or two sets of 8 to 12 reps, pick a weight that you can curl—with both arms at the same time—for 7 to 8 reps with moderate effort.
- On the eighth, ninth, and tenth reps, you should really have to push yourself.
- Once you've picked that weight, use this weight for all 10 sets of 10 reps.
- While seated on the bench with your upper body erect, bring your arms straight down to your sides until they are straight.
- You can also do these with one arm resting on top of your leg, much like a seated concentration curl.
- Make sure your palms face straight out in front of you and straight up toward the ceiling as you curl the weight up.

For this exercise, keep palms up from start to finish.

- Begin curling the weight up, and as you do, stop the dumbbells about three-fourths of the way up or at shoulder level. Find the position where your biceps are peak contracted.
- Once you reach this position, slowly bring your elbows straight up and out in front of you for an even greater peak contraction.
- Hold this peak contraction for a brief second, and while keeping

your arms in this position, slowly lower the weight until your arms are fully extended.

- As your arms almost reach the fully extended position, you can slowly lower your upper arms down and back to your sides until they reach the starting position.
- Do 10 sets of 10 reps.
- Allow only a one-second peak contraction rest between reps.
- Do not rest any longer than 45 seconds between sets.

If you do these like I've just described, you will feel the most intense burn you have ever felt! That's the whole key to making your biceps grow and get stronger; you have to peak contract and not allow them to rest very long before you hit them again. Remember, make the muscles work harder by creating intensity in every exercise and workout you do.

After you've done 10 sets of 10 reps of these three exercises, you're finished, so get the heck out of the gym. Drink a can of fruit juice to replenish that used muscle glycogen, and have a good protein meal within 40 to 90 minutes of your workout. Get plenty of rest, take the next day off from any and all training, and 48 hours later, you'll be ready for your second workout of 10 sets of 10 reps. Then get ready . . . because your body is about to explode with new growth and strength.

13

Workout 6: The 10 System, Part III

If you've followed the 10 System the way I've told you in the last two chapters, you should be noticing some pretty incredible things. Your strength should be increasing, your body should feel like you've really put it through a workout, you should see and feel your muscles changing size and shape, and you should be eating like a horse! What you've been doing is putting a physical and mental demand on your body that it hasn't been used to. You've shocked it and the only way it knows how to respond to 10 sets of 10 reps is by growing and getting stronger. Now, that must be good news to you.

This chapter I'm going to give you the next 10 System workout. But before I do, let's review the first two 10 System workouts.

You should use the 10 System for only one week for every 8 to 10 weeks of training. During this one week, you will only do these three exercises—and no others. You will do 10 sets of 10 reps for each exercise three times during that one week with a complete day of

rest between workouts (for example, Monday–Wednesday–Friday).

You can use the 10 System all year round; however, each time you use it (one week for every 8 to 10 weeks of training), use different exercises and work different bodyparts. Here's the first workout to show what I mean.

- 8 to 10 weeks of regular training
- Then one week of three workouts using three exercises of 10 sets of 10 reps
- First 10 System workout will be squats, chin-ups, and shoulder presses

This is what your first 8 to 10 weeks of regular training and first workout using the 10 System would be. Now, after the next 8 to 10 weeks of regular training, here's what I wanted you to do on the 10 System second workout.

- Chest—30-degree incline dumbbell press, 10 sets of 10 reps
- Hamstrings—stiff-legged barbell or dumbbell deadlift, (preferably on a wooden platform), 10 sets of 10 reps

Partner-assisted donkey calf raises are phenomenal.

- Biceps—seated palms-up dumbbell curl, three-fourths range of movement, 10 sets of 10 reps

For the third 10 System workout, we will focus on calves, triceps, and forearms. Ready to get blastin'?

CALVES

Donkey Calf Raise with Partner on Your Lower Back and with Toes on Four-Inch-High Wood Block

You should do calves first because very few people who work out have great calves. One of the reasons for this, besides genetics, is they work their calves at the very end of their workouts and they don't do the best exercises for them. But that's all about to change.

The calf exercise you will do is donkey calf raises, but not on a machine. You must have a partner sit

on your lower back while you do these. The stretch and burn you will feel will be incredible. Here's how to do them.

- Place your toes and the balls of your feet on a four-inch block of wood.
- Be sure the block of wood is high enough so you can lower your heels all the way down for a full stretch and not touch the floor.
- While keeping your legs straight and knees locked, bend your upper body over until it is at a 90-degree angle.
- To support your upper body, rest your forearms and elbows on a flat bench or rack of dumbbells.
- Have your training partner sit on top of your lower back. His or her body should be centered almost at the very end of your lower back in a position where his or her body should be right above your glutes and legs.
- The farther back your partner sits, the more you will feel the stretch in your calves.
- Slowly lower your heels for a good stretch and hold there for one to two seconds, then slowly raise your heels up until you are on the tips of your toes.
- Hold there for one to two seconds, then slowly lower your heels again and repeat until you've done 10 reps.
- Rest for no longer than 30 to 45 seconds, and do the set again until you've done 10 sets of 10 reps.
- After you've done 10 sets of 10 reps, with your partner still on your back, simply lower your heels again and keep your legs and knees locked out and stretch your calves in that position for 30 to 60 seconds. Talk about a major burn!

TRICEPS

Seated Dumbbell French Press with Palms Up

The second exercise of the workout is for your triceps, the biggest part of your arms. The key to really feeling this exercise is making sure your elbows are fully warmed up. Don't use the heavy iron until those elbows and triceps tendons have been warmed up with at least 2 to 3 sets of 15 to 20 reps of triceps pressdowns or push-ups and 1 to 2 sets of light (40 to 50 percent of your max weight) seated dumbbell-behind-head French presses. You must take a few extra minutes to do this in order to avoid any injury and get the most from this exercise.

Once you feel your triceps are ready, here's what you need to do.

- Pick a dumbbell you can do for 10 reps, but on the eight or ninth rep, you will need to push yourself a bit.
- Find a seated bench with preferably a small back support. Those smaller seated benches for doing presses or curls work great.
- Be sure the back support will allow you to lower the dumbbell all the way down behind your head without the dumbbell hitting the back support and stopping you from doing a full range of movement.
- Grasp the dumbbell with both hands so that your hands are clasped together and your palms are turned up to face the ceiling.
- While keeping your upper arms close to your head, raise the dumbbell above your head and slowly lower the weight all the way down behind your head until your triceps are fully stretched.
- Raise the dumbbell back up over your head until your arms are completely locked out.

Dumbbell French presses are like squats for your triceps.

- Squeeze your triceps hard for an intense contraction.
- Slowly lower the weight and repeat until you've done 10 reps.
- Rest no longer than 45 to 60 seconds, and repeat the exercise until you've done 10 sets of 10 reps.
- Once you've finished, raise one arm above your head and allow your forearm to come back behind you while you keep your upper arm close to your head, as this will stretch your triceps. Be sure to do it for 10 to 20 seconds for each arm.

FOREARMS

Seated Barbell Roll-Off and Roll-Up with Legs Locking Arms

The third and final exercise you will do for this workout is for your forearms. I put forearms last for a special reason: they are already warmed up from all the triceps work you just did, so they're ready for the heavy weight.

You can do many different forearm exercises, but one of the very best is using a barbell off of a flat bench. To really feel it, you need to position your body just right. Here's how.

- Choose a barbell with a thinner bar, such as a chrome barbell. Try to stay away from a regular-width Olympic or powerlifter-type barbell. You want the barbell to roll off your fingers (which I'll soon explain).
- With a barbell in your hands, sit down on a flat bench.

- Keep your forearms and elbows on the flat bench at all times. Never allow them to come up off the bench.
- Be sure that only your wrists and hands are hanging off over the end of the bench.
- Squeeze your legs together so they are bracing your forearms on the bench.
- Now, with the barbell in your hands, slowly open your hands and let the barbell roll down until it reaches the ends of your fingers.
- Once it does that, slowly roll the barbell back up into your palms and close your hands as you bring your hands as far as you can toward your forearms.
- Hold the barbell in this fully contracted forearm position for two to three seconds, then slowly lower it again and repeat.
- Do this for 10 reps.
- After you've done 10 sets of 10 reps, place the palms of your hands against a wall and raise your arms higher than your hands and hold it there for 20 to 30 seconds. This will stretch your forearms.

Great job, you're now finished with your workout. So get your stuff and get out of the gym. Grab a can of fruit juice on the way home. Eat a good protein meal within 40 to 90 minutes, and get some rest. You deserve it. Your body can now grow and be ready for the next 10 System workout.

The next chapter will present the last 10 System workout, and I'm going to give you a surprise that you're going to like.

14

Workout 7: The 10 System, Part IV

Well, your body has been put through three different 10 System workouts and it's ready for the fourth and final one. But before we get into it, and before I reveal the surprise, let's quickly review the previous 10 System workouts.

You should use the 10 System for only one week for every 8 to 10 weeks of training. During this one week, you will only do these three exercises—and no others—you will do 10 sets of 10 reps for each exercise three times during that one week with a complete day of rest between workouts (for example, Monday–Wednesday–Friday).

You can use the 10 System all year round; however, each time you use it (one week for every 8 to 10 weeks of training), use different exercises and work different bodyparts. Here's the first workout to show what I mean.

- 8 to 10 weeks of regular training
- Then one week of three workouts using three exercises of 10 sets of 10 reps

- First 10 System workout will be squats, chin-ups, and shoulder presses

This is what your first 8 to 10 weeks of regular training and first workout using the 10 System would be. Now, after the next 8 to 10 weeks of regular training, here's what I wanted you to do on the 10 System second workout.

- Chest—30-degree incline dumbbell press, 10 sets of 10 reps
- Hamstrings—Stiff-legged barbell or dumbbell deadlift (preferably on a wooden platform), 10 sets of 10 reps
- Biceps—Seated palms-up dumbbell curl, three-fourths range of movement, 10 sets of 10 reps

After the next 8 to 10 weeks of training, here's what I wanted you to do for the third 10 System workout:

- Calves—Donkey calf raise with partner on your lower back and with toes on four-inch-high wood block, 10 sets of 10 reps
- Triceps—Seated dumbbell-behind-head French press with palms up, 10 sets of 10 reps
- Forearms—Seated barbell roll-off and roll-up with legs locking arms, 10 sets of 10 reps

OK, the fourth 10 System workout will focus on abs, traps, and a killer biceps/triceps superset that will put major size on your arms in a hurry. But first things first: abs.

ABS

Seated Crunch with Training Partner Holding Your Calves Against Top of Flat Bench

Most people think crunches are a good exercise for shaping up the midsection,

and they are right. However, if you *really* want to feel it, do your crunches in the following very special way.

- Lie down on your back with your knees bent and your calves resting on top of a flat bench.
- Have a training partner either hold your ankles down against the bench or have him or her sit on top of your calves and ankles while you do the exercise.
- Fold your arms across your chest or clasp your hands together behind your head.
- Roll your upper torso forward and crunch, and come up as high as you can.
- At the top position, hold your body in that crunched position for one to two seconds, and very slowly allow your upper torso to come back down and straighten out.

Great abs come from itelligent ab training, a healthy diet, and genetics.

- You're only going to allow it to unroll and come back down slightly, however, as you want to keep constant tension on the abs.
- Keep your upper torso elevated and off the floor at the bottom position, and be sure to hold it there for one to two seconds before crunching and coming back up again.
- The trick to really feeling this exercise is to do very slow reps and keep your upper body up and off the floor at all times.
- Rest only 25 to 35 seconds between sets.
- Do 10 sets of 10 reps.

TRAPS

Barbell Shrugs with Static Holds

Who hasn't seen a powerful looking physique that didn't have big traps? They all do, because they do deadlifts and shrugs. But I'm about to show you a way to do shrugs that will pack on slabs of muscle on those traps. Here's how.

- The best place to do shrugs is in a power rack. If you can use a power rack, great. If not, then do regular shrugs with a barbell on the floor.
- Using a rack, set the rack bar so the barbell rests at knee level. This will be the starting position.
- After a 1 to 2 set warm-up with a lighter weight, go ahead and load the barbell with a weight that you can do for a tough 10 reps. In other words, don't make it too heavy, but also not too light.
- Take a medium grip—about shoulder-width—on the barbell. You can have both hands in an overhand grip or a combination of one hand over and the other hand under.

- Keeping your legs slightly bent and upper body erect, with arms locked out, raise your shoulders straight up toward the ceiling.
- Don't row your shoulders from front to back. Just raise them straight up and down.
- At the top of the movement, hold the barbell for one to two seconds and slowly lower it back to the starting position.
- Do 10 reps, rest 30 to 60 seconds, and do another set until you've done 10 sets of 10 reps.
- On your last two sets (the ninth and tenth ones), I want you to do something a bit different on the eighth, ninth, and tenth reps. Instead of lowering the barbell all the way down and then shrugging it straight up like you've been doing, set the barbell down and shrug your shoulders all the way up, then grab the barbell and hold it at the top position, and then slowly lower it.
- You are simply doing half reps starting with the barbell in the top position and slowly lowering it, then setting it down in the rack and grabbing it again with your shoulders in the top position, and starting again. You'll definitely feel a great burn!

BICEPS AND TRICEPS, SUPERSET

Thumbs-Up Dumbbell Curls to Lying EZ-Bar French Press Away from Head

I promised a surprise for you and here it is: a great superset that will pump your arms up like a balloon. Do them like this:

- You will begin with biceps, and you'll use the thumbs-up dumbbell curl.

Thumbs-up curls give your biceps more fullness.

- Do the curls with both arms simultaneously.
- To work the brachialis (the muscle that sits under the biceps) and biceps at the same time, sit at the end of a flat bench and keep your upper torso erect.

Lying EZ-bar French press: the weight should be lowered below your head and extended behind you.

- While holding the dumbbells in each hand, keep your thumbs up and palms facing each other.
- Curl the weights up and as the dumbbells get closer to your shoulders, start turning the wrists so that your thumbs turn out and away from your body.
- Be sure to contract your biceps hard at the top of the movement and hold that contraction for one to two seconds before lowering the weights.
- As you lower the weights, turn your wrists again so that your thumbs face up and your palms face each other.
- Do 10 reps.
- Put the dumbbells down, and immediately grab the EZ-bar with a narrow grip and lie down.
- Raise your arms over your body, then bring them back over and behind your head.
- Keeping your upper arms at a 45-degree angle behind your head, bend your elbows and allow your hands and forearms to come down below your head.
- While keeping your upper arms at that 45-degree angle and never moving them, move only your forearms and hands and bring the weight back up behind your head and lock out the elbows.
- You must keep your arms behind your head—not over it, doing nose crunchers like so many other people do. This is the only way you'll really get the best results from this exercise.
- Do 10 reps.
- As soon as you're finished with the triceps exercise, rest 30 to 45 seconds and do the thumbs-up dumbbell curls again followed by the triceps exercise.
- Do these back-to-back with minimal rest in between sets so you'll

get the maximum burn and best results.

- Do a total of 10 sets of 10 reps.
- I guarantee if you do these two exercises exactly like I've told you, your arms will be screaming.

So there you have it. Four 10 System workouts that will shock your body into growth like it hasn't seen since you were a beginner. And while your week of 10 System workouts will probably be some of the toughest training you've ever done, you'll be rewarded with new growth, strength, endurance, and a mental toughness unlike anything you've experienced.

This is the wrong way to do a lying EZ-bar French press. The weight should extend out and behind your head.

15

Workout 8: The Back-to-Front System

What you're about to learn in this chapter and in Chapter 16 is a workout very few people do, mainly because most people never heard of it or don't know how to do it correctly. But for those who do, and you'll soon be one of them, it will give you incredible results and an equally incredible pump like you've never felt before!

The workout is in two parts, back-to-front and top-to-bottom. Before we get started, there are a few things you must know and do in order to get the most powerful results from it.

- You will only do this workout four days a week—for example, Monday, Tuesday, Thursday, and Friday. Take Wednesday, Saturday, and Sunday off from training.
- You will do superset-only bodypart training, with your bodyparts being worked as follows:
  - Chest to back
  - Biceps to triceps
  - Hamstrings to quads
  - Lower back to abs
  - Shoulders to calves
- You will only do two exercises per bodypart.

- You will only do 4 sets per exercise and 8 sets total per bodypart.
- The reps you will use will vary depending on what bodypart you are training.
- The rest between sets will be no longer than 45 seconds.
- The first exercise superset you will do for each bodypart will be your heaviest exercise, hitting those deep-growth muscle fibers.
- The second exercise superset you will do for each bodypart will be light in order to pump blood through your muscles and flush the lactic acid from the worked muscle so it can grow and recover more quickly and efficiently.
- For cardio training, do the stationary bike, treadmill, or stair stepper for no longer than 10 to 12 minutes *before* you weight train. Do it at a brisk pace in order to get your blood flowing and heart rate up.
- After cardio training, rest no longer than two minutes before you begin hitting the weights. Doing this will keep your heart

rate and metabolism elevated throughout your entire workout.

- A very important thing you need to concentrate on is the mind-muscle link. Close your eyes whenever you can, and feel and visualize the muscle work as you intensely contract the muscle while you're lifting the weight.

- Have each rep make the muscle work harder and harder. You'll be amazed at how quickly you can make your muscles grow and get stronger by doing this. Using your mind is *extremely* important in helping you get bigger and stronger, and quickly changing how you look and feel the *fastest* way possible.

- You will do the back-to-front workout system for three weeks and then take one complete week off from any kind of training.

- After your week off from training, go back to your regular training routine.

- You can use the back-to-front system once every three months.

So if you're ready for an incredible workout that will amaze you, let's get started by doing chest and back, then biceps and triceps.

CHEST-TO-BACK FIRST EXERCISE SUPERSET (HEAVY): INCLINE DUMBBELL PRESS TO T-BAR OR DUMBBELL ROW

Incline Dumbbell Press

I prefer that you do these on an incline bench that is elevated at a 25- to 35-degree angle, slightly below the normal incline angle you see on most benches in gyms. The 25- to 35-degree angle seems to work great because it hits the chest and minimizes the participation of the shoulder muscles.

Always make your first set a light warm-up set. Do 8 to 12 reps and really

Begin with 10 to 12 minutes of cardio to get your heart rate up.

After a warm-up set, begin your chest-to-back superset with the incline dumbbell press.

stretch your chest by allowing the dumbbells to come down as low as possible. If you feel like you need it, go ahead and do another warm-up set. After a good warm-up set, you're ready to begin the chest-to-back superset.

Pick a weight that you can do for 6 to 8 reps. Since you're already warmed up, go right to your heaviest set. Do 6 to 8 reps and make sure you lower the weights far enough so you get a great chest stretch. Always control the weight and don't do fast reps. Normal steady-pace reps do the trick. As soon as you've done your set, rack the weight and immediately do the second exercise in the superset, the T-bar or dumbbell row.

T-Bar or Dumbbell Row

It is preferable that you do T-bar rows, but if you can't, then dumbbell rows will do. If you do the T-bars, you should again use a weight that will allow you to do 6 to 8 reps. To get the most from this exercise, you need to do a few things:

- Keep your knees slightly bent and keep your upper body at a 90-degree angle to the floor.
- Use a close grip.
- Keep your body in this position during the entire exercise; use only your arms to pull the weight up and down.
- Always pull the weight up until it touches your chest, then lower it all the way down until your arms are fully extended and you get the maximum lat stretch.
- After you've done 6 to 8 reps, rest no longer than 50 seconds before doing your second superset.

For the next three supersets, use this same weight for the T-bars. However, for the incline press for the chest, reduce the weight by about 10 percent for each of the next three sets.

Let the weight come all the way down as your upper body remains stationary.

For example, the first set do 100 pounds, the second set use 90 pounds, the third set use 80 pounds, and the fourth set use 70 pounds.

CHEST-TO-BACK SECOND EXERCISE SUPERSET (LIGHT): DUMBBELL FLYE TO CHIN-UP OR WIDE-GRIP MACHINE PULLDOWN

Your chest and back should feel like you've really hit the deep fibers. Now it's time for the finishing touch and the incredible pump. We'll start the second exercise superset with the chest, this time doing dumbbell flyes.

Dumbbell Flyes

Pick a weight that you can do for 10 to 12 reps. Don't use a heavy weight. Now, we are only interested in pumping the muscle. Using a slightly inclined flat bench tends to work great for this exercise. With a dumbbell in each hand,

You don't need heavy weights to make flyes work their magic.

As the bar comes down to your upper chest, slightly arch your back.

slowly lower the weight out to your sides and away from your body. Your arms should be almost fully extended but with a slight bend at the elbows. Get a really good stretch.

As you bring the weights back up to the starting position at the top, do not press the weight as if you were doing a dumbbell bench press. The flye is much different. Bring the weights up in a big arc or circle—like you're putting your arms around a big barrel—until you reach the top position with the weights above your head. After you've done 10 to 12 reps, then put the weights down and quickly move to your next exercise, the chin-up or wide-grip machine pulldown.

Chin-Up or Wide-Grip Machine Pulldown

The best exercise would be the chin-up. So go over to the chinning bar and place your hands about 8 to 10 inches wider than your shoulders. Begin by keeping your upper body straight and your legs bent with your feet behind you. Pull yourself all the way up until your chin is above the bar. As you pull yourself up, you can slightly arch your back and allow your chest to

come forward. After you reach the top, slowly lower yourself until your arms are fully extended and do your next rep. Do as many reps as possible.

For the next three supersets, use the same weight and reps for the dumbbell flye and do chin-ups the same way you did your first set. Rest no longer than 35 to 45 seconds between sets.

After you've done eight supersets for your chest and back, take a three-to-four-minute rest and you'll be ready to hit biceps and triceps.

BICEPS-TO-TRICEPS FIRST EXERCISE SUPERSET (HEAVY): SEATED DUMB-BELL INCLINE CURL TO MACHINE PRESSDOWN WITH STRAIGHT BAR

Seated Dumbbell Incline Curl

A 45-degree angled bench will work fine for this exercise. After you've done

Arnold Schwarzenegger loved this exercise—do it right and you will too.

Machine Pressdown with Straight Bar

Start your first set with a moderate weight, and you'll increase the weight on each of the next three sets. This is to make sure that your triceps tendon is fully warmed once you hit the heaviest weight.

Place your hands about 8 to 10 inches apart on the straight bar. Lock your upper arms and elbows close into your sides and only move your lower arms and elbows while you do the exercise. Allow the bar to come no higher than chest level, and be sure to fully extend your arms and contract the triceps hard as you press the weight down. Do 9 to 11 reps.

Rest no longer than 45 seconds between sets. Increase the weight for each exercise by 10 percent each set. For example, use 30 pounds on the first set of incline curls, then go up

a light warm-up set of standing dumbbell curls, pick heavy enough weights that you can do for only 6 to 8 reps.

Keep your back and head against the backpad and your glutes planted firmly on the seat. Let your arms hang down to your sides. With your thumbs up and your palms facing each other, curl the weights up, turning the weights up as you turn your wrists until your palms face upward. Be sure to keep your elbows in one position and close to the bench throughout the exercise. Bring the weights up until they are at shoulder level. You must find the place at the top of the curl where you feel the greatest biceps contraction. Each person is different, so really concentrate and find the right spot for you. Slowly lower the weights until your arms are fully extended, and continue with your next rep until you've done 6 to 8 reps. After you've done 6 to 8 reps, immediately put the weights down—*never drop them!*—and move to the next exercise.

Keep your arms close to the body and squeeze for maximum contraction.

to 35 pounds on your second set, 40 pounds on your third, and 45 pounds on your fourth. After doing four supersets, you can rest three to four minutes before moving to the last biceps and triceps superset.

BICEPS-TO-TRICEPS SECOND EXERCISE SUPERSET (LIGHT): BARBELL PREACHER CURL TO LYING EZ-BAR FRENCH PRESS

Barbell Preacher Curl

Now we're ready to pump the biceps and triceps. Start with barbell preacher curls, which will work the lower biceps and give you a lot of fullness down there.

Do these on the side of the bench that has a slight angle and not the 90-degree steep side of the bench. Take a

Stop the weight when the biceps reach peak contraction, about three-fourths of the way up.

barbell that's light enough for you to do 18 to 22 reps. You will do high reps on these, so don't worry about using heavy weights.

Take a shoulder-width grip and place your elbows on the bench so they are only 8 to 10 inches apart. Remember, your elbows must be narrower than your grip. Hands out and elbows in. Lower the weight until your arms are fully extended. Don't hyperextend your elbows by lowering the weight so quickly that it injures your tendons and elbows. Slow and steady is the key. Once your arms are fully extended, slowly curl the weight up until your biceps are fully contracted. Do not allow the weight to come up to the top and then fall back toward your shoulders. If that happens, you've gone too far and you've passed the point of maximal biceps contraction. Once you've done 18 to 22 reps, put the weight down and immediately do a set of lying EZ-bar French presses.

Lying EZ-Bar French Press

Use a flat bench for this one and choose a weight—preferably using the EZ-bar—that you can do for 20 reps. Take a close grip on the EZ-bar and lie down. Fully extend your arms until the weight is above your head. Bring your arms and the weight behind your head. Your upper arms should be at about a 45-degree angle behind your head. Keeping your upper arms in this position during the entire exercise, slowly lower the weight down behind and below your head in order to get a great triceps stretch. Then bring your hands, forearms, and the weight up until your arms are fully locked out and your triceps are fully contracted.

Do not do nose crunchers! That is, don't keep your upper arms straight up and down at a 90-degree angle and lower the weight down to your face. Most people do this exercise this way, but it's not nearly as effective as the way I have described. If you do this exercise the way I have instucted you to, you'll be amazed at how quickly your triceps will grow!

Next chapter, we'll turn to the complementary workout, the top-to-bottom system, with exercises for hamstrings, quads, lower back, abs, shoulders, and calves.

For lying French presses, the EZ-bar works best.

16

Workout 9: The Top-to-Bottom System

In the last chapter you learned the workout called back-to-front that very few people do, yet as you no doubt have experienced, that gives you an incredible pump and fabulous results.

In this chapter you will learn the top-to-bottom system. But before you do, let's review the key things you must remember.

- You will only do this workout four days a week. For example, Monday, Tuesday, Thursday, and Friday. Take Wednesday, Saturday, and Sunday off from training.
- You will do superset-only bodypart training, with your bodyparts being worked as follows:
  - Chest to back
  - Biceps to triceps
  - Hamstrings to quads
  - Lower back to abs
  - Shoulders to calves
- You will only do two exercises per bodypart.
- You will only do 4 sets per exercise and 8 sets total per bodypart.

- The reps you will use will vary depending on what bodypart you are training.
- The rest between sets will be no longer than 45 seconds.
- The first exercise superset you will do for each bodypart will be your heaviest exercise, hitting those deep-growth muscle fibers.
- The second exercise superset you will do for each bodypart will be light in order to pump blood through your muscles and flush the lactic acid from the worked muscle so it can grow and recover more quickly and efficiently.
- For cardio training, do the stationary bike, treadmill, or stair stepper for no longer than 10 to 12 minutes *before* you weight train. Do it at a brisk pace in order to get your blood flowing and heart rate up.
- After cardio training, rest no longer than two minutes before you begin hitting the weights. Doing this will keep your heart rate and metabolism elevated throughout your entire workout.

- A very important thing you need to concentrate on is the mind–muscle link. Close your eyes whenever you can, and feel and visualize the muscle work as you intensely contract the muscle while you're lifting the weight.
- Have each rep make the muscle work harder and harder. You'll be amazed at how quickly you can make your muscles grow and get stronger by doing this. Using your mind is *extremely* important in helping you get bigger and stronger the fastest way possible.
- You will do the top-to-bottom workout system for three weeks and then take one complete week off from any kind of training.
- After your week off from training, go back to your regular training routine.
- You can use the top-to-bottom system once every three months.

HAMSTRINGS-TO-QUADS FIRST EXERCISE SUPERSET (HEAVY): STIFF-LEGGED DEADLIFT TO LEG PRESS

Stiff-Legged Deadlift

I prefer that you do these with a barbell; however, you can use dumbbells. Also, you'll get a better stretch if you do these standing on an elevated platform or bench.

Take a barbell with a weight heavy enough that you can do 6 reps. Use either an overhand grip or a one-hand-over/one-hand-under grip. Be sure your grip is about shoulder width. With a slight bend at your knees, slowly lower the barbell down until you feel a good stretch in your hamstrings. For some people, this may be at shin level; for others, it may be all the way down until the weight touches the tops of their shoes. Keep your back slightly arched and your head looking forward and

For the best stretch, lower the weight to shin level or lower.

Keep the back slightly arched throughout the exercise.

straight ahead. Keep the barbell close to your body during the entire exercise. As you bring the weight up, bend only your upper torso and stop when your upper body is in a straight line with your legs. After you've done 6 reps, put the weight down and immediately go to leg presses.

Leg Press

Pick a weight that you'll be able to do for 8 to 10 reps. Place your feet on the platform with a wide stance and your toes angled slightly outward. Stay tight in the seat, and don't let your glutes come up and off the seat when you lower the weight. Lower the weight down until your knees are near shoulder level and out and away from your body. Always keep your knees in a direct line over your big toes when either lowering or pushing the weight. Do 8 to 10 nonstop reps.

Rest no longer than 45 seconds between sets. Use the same weight on each exercise for all 4 sets. After you've done 4 supersets, rest no more than 60 seconds before you do the second superset for legs.

SECOND EXERCISE SUPERSET (LIGHT): LEG CURL TO LEG EXTENSION

Leg Curl

Now we're going for reps. Start off with the lying leg curl. Be sure to keep your stomach tight and against the pad as

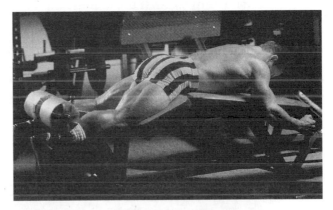

Keep hips and legs on the pads at all times

With the leg press, allow the weight to come all the way down and do nonstop reps.

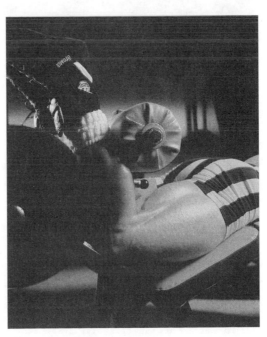

Bring the ankle pads toward the glutes until you feel the hamstring maximally contract.

you do these. Always do full-range-of-motion reps: full stretch when you extend your legs and a good contraction as you curl the weight up toward your glutes. And always keep the reps going by not stopping until you've finished all your reps for the set. Do 20 reps.

Leg Extension

After you've done 20 reps of leg curls, immediately begin a set of leg extensions and do 20 reps. Be sure to keep the backs of your legs (around the knee area) firmly against the seat.

Bring your upper body forward and lean over your quads while you do these. Fully extend your legs in front of you and squeeze really hard as you contract the muscles. Hold your legs in this contracted position for one to two seconds, then slowly lower your legs down and repeat.

For extra burn, bring your upper body forward and lean over your quads.

Rest no longer than 30 seconds between sets. After you've done 4 supersets, you can rest three to four minutes before doing the lower-back-to-abs superset.

LOWER-BACK-TO-ABS HYPEREXTENSION TO CRUNCH

Hyperextension

This is the only back-to-front superset with only one superset and not two. The reason is that on the previous superset for hamstrings and quads, you've already thoroughly worked your lower back by doing the stiff-legged deadlifts. You don't want to overtrain it, so you will do the hyperextension as a great finishing exercise.

On a hyper bench, position your upper body so it doesn't touch the bench. You want it to move freely. With your arms in front of you tucked near your chest, bend your upper torso until your head is near the floor. Hold this position for one to two seconds. Then slowly raise your upper torso until it is even and in a direct line with your legs. Do not hyperextend your upper body by allowing it to rise higher than your legs. After doing 12 to 15 reps, immediately do a set of crunches.

Hyperextension can be a fabulous hamstring, glute, and lower back exercise.

Crunch

You probably have done a crunch at some point in your training. However, many people do them wrong. The right way to do them is by using only a slight range of movement and doing a lot of reps with minimal rest between sets.

As you do the crunch, bring your upper body forward and crunch the abs as far as possible; then only allow the body to come back down about three to four inches before you come back forward and crunch the abs again. Many people come forward and then allow their upper bodies to come all the way down to the floor before they start again. This is not very effective. The abs work best with constant tension kept on them, so the method I've told you will really make them work! Do 30 to 40 reps.

Rest no longer than 30 seconds between sets. Once you've done four supersets, you'll be ready to work your shoulders and calves.

SHOULDERS-TO-CALVES FIRST EXERCISE SUPERSET (HEAVY): ONE-ARM STANDING DUMBBELL PRESS OR SEATED MACHINE PRESS TO STANDING CALF RAISE

One-Arm Standing Dumbbell Press or Seated Machine Press

This is a great mass builder. The movement is very similar to the regular dumbbell press except you do the exercise only one arm at a time instead of two.

After a good set or two of warm-ups, pick a weight that will allow you to do 5 to 7 reps. I suggest you do this

To make the crunch most effective, use a very slight range of motion.

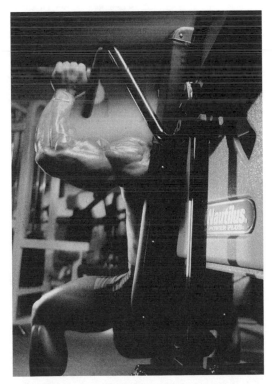

Delts respond incredibly well to nonstop, nonlockout reps with minimal rest between sets.

exercise standing with a weight in one hand and with your other hand holding onto the top of a bench for support. Bring the weight all the way up above your head and fully extend your arm. Bring the weight back down and lower it until the side of the dumbbell is at shoulder level. Always go for the full extension at the top and the full stretch at the bottom. After you've done 5 to 7 reps, go immediately to the standing calf raise.

Standing Calf Raise

You're probably familiar with this exercise, too. You must remember the stretch at the bottom and the contraction at the top of the movement. Your calves get worked every single day through walking. If you weigh 150 pounds, your calves get 150 pounds of resistance with each step, but they don't get 150 pounds of resistance

Calves can become cows when you contract them all the way up and stretch them all the way down.

in the full range where growth is stimulated.

Place the balls of your feet on the ends of the platform. Keep your body erect and only move your feet and ankles throughout the exercise. Pick a weight that is at least 50 percent heavier than your bodyweight and do 10 to 12 reps per set. Allow the weight to lower your heels all the way down to the floor below the platform in order to get a great stretch. Hold the weight in this position for one to two seconds; then raise up on your toes until your calves are fully contracted at the top position.

Rest no longer than 30 seconds between sets. After you've done four supersets, rest for three to four minutes before doing the second and final superset.

SECOND EXERCISE SUPERSET (LIGHT): DUMBBELL SIDE OR BENT-OVER LATERAL TO LEG PRESS TOE RAISE

Dumbbell Side or Bent-Over Lateral

The trick to making the delts work hard is not so much using heavy weights, but keeping the delts moving and working with little rest between reps and sets. You want to make them burn!

Take a pair of dumbbells that you can do 14 to 16 reps with, and either sit down on a flat bench or stand. Allow the weights to come down to your sides but don't let them touch your body. Keep them about 6 to 10 inches out and away from your body. This is the starting position.

Raise the weights up and directly out to your sides. Keep the weights in a direct line with your upper body. Bring the weights up only as high as your shoulders and hold them there for one to two seconds. Slowly lower the

Use more weight if you are able to do so without compromising your form.

weights back down and repeat. After you've done 14 to 16 reps, go immediately to leg press toe raises.

Leg Press Toe Raise

Use only enough weight to where you can do 30 reps. You really want to make your calves scream on this one. Sit in the seat like you would if you were doing a regular leg press. Instead of placing your feet high up on the platform, place the balls of your feet on the very lower edge or bottom of the platform. *Keep your knees completely straight—this is very important!* (If you have weak knees, a slight bend is OK, but the straighter the knee, the more productive this exercise is.) Let the weight come down a few inches until your toes come back as far as possible. This is the bottom or the fully stretched position. Hold the weight there for one to two seconds, then push the weight up with your feet until your calves are fully contracted and will not go any

Let the weight come down until your toes are pushed back as far as possible.

farther. Do 30 reps and rest only 30 seconds between sets.

After you've done four supersets, stretch your calves as follows:

- Find a platform that will allow you to lower your heels as far down as possible without touching the floor.

- Stay in this fully stretched position for at least 50 seconds.
- Do this after every calf workout and watch what happens to your calves!

If you follow this top-to-bottom workout exactly, you will get incredible results.

17

Workout 10: The 12/12 Workout

Many people I know have less than an hour a day to work out. They have asked, "Is there anything I can do that'll give my body both an effective weight and aerobic workout?" Absolutely!

How many times have you read or heard that you must train aerobically for at least 30 minutes three times a week to get any real benefits? Or that you must weight train for 30 minutes or do a certain number of sets and reps? When well-intentioned people make these kinds of must-do claims, they are lumping everyone in the same pile, thinking everyone will not benefit unless they follow those guidelines.

But you and I know that's not the case. Even though we are all human, the results each of us gets from what we do and the time it takes for each of us to do it can vary widely. What I'm about to give you flies right in the face of those who say you can't get any appreciable aerobic benefits unless you're spending a lot of time on the treadmill, bike, or stair stepper. You'll probably like it because it only takes 24

minutes, and you can be in and out of the gym in less than 30 minutes.

WHAT YOU MUST KNOW

- You'll do this workout three times per week; pick any three days you want. I suggest leaving a day of rest between each day of workouts; for example, work out Monday, rest Tuesday, work out Wednesday, rest Thursday, work out Friday, and rest Saturday and Sunday.
- One day begin with cardio, then do weights; on the next workout, switch things around and begin with weights and finish with cardio.
- The key to making this brief cardio and weight training very effective is not to rest more than 30 to 45 seconds between sets and exercises.
- As soon as you finish your cardio workout, immediately start on the weight training workout.

- The combination of these two types of training will keep your heart rate elevated throughout the entire 24-minute workout, and thereby give you a super metabolism-elevating and endurance-benefit result. It will also keep you stronger, leaner, firmer, tighter, and looking good.

SAMPLE WORKOUT PLAN (MONDAY)

Cardio—Brisk Walking on Treadmill, 12 Minutes

- Begin with the treadmill at 0 degrees of elevation (flat) and set the treadmill speed to 3.5 to 3.7 mph.
- Take long strides, with your upper torso and head erect and looking forward.
- With each stride, swing your arms up and out in front and behind

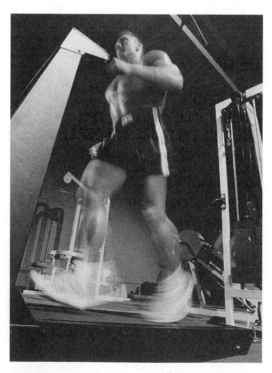

Take big, long strides and move those arms back and forth.

you in rhythm. Think big movements for the arms and legs.

- At the two-minute mark, raise the treadmill elevation to between 3 and 5 degrees (depending on difficulty) and increase the treadmill speed to 3.8 to 4.0 mph.
- At the six-minute mark, raise the treadmill elevation to between 7 and 10 degrees (depending on difficulty) and keep the treadmill speed between 3.8 and 4.0 mph.
- At the 10-minute mark, lower the treadmill elevation to 5 degrees and reduce the speed to 3.5 mph.
- At the 11-minute mark, lower the treadmill to 0-degree elevation (flat) and reduce the speed to 3.0 mph.
- At the 12-minute mark, stop and get off. You're finished.

Weights—the One-Set-per-Bodypart Workout

By the time you get to the weight training portion of the workout, you'll be warmed up enough to immediately work your legs. Remember, you're only going to do one set per bodypart and that's it.

- Leg extension: do 1 set to failure, but pick a weight (not too heavy or light) that you can do for at least 15 reps.
- Lying leg curl: do 1 set to failure and same as above.
- Standing calf raise, machine or bodyweight only: do 1 set of 20 to 40 reps.
- Chest—pec deck/seated hammer press or machine bench press: do 1 set of 10 to 13 reps.
- Shoulders and delts—standing barbell press: do 1 set of 12 to 14 reps.
- Triceps—machine pressdown with straight bar: do 1 set of 15 to 18 reps.

When you're only doing one set, make each rep your best one.

Cable crossovers are one of the most underrated but effective chest exercises.

- Back—wide-grip front pulldown (to upper chest just under the neck): do 1 set of 14 to 18 reps.
- Biceps—barbell or dumbbell curl (both arms at the same time, standing or seated): do 1 set of 12 to 20 reps.
- Abs—crunch (with knees elevated): do 1 set of 40 to 60 reps.
- Stretch—work all body groups with additional emphasis on any areas you want.
- You're finished.

SAMPLE WORKOUT PLAN (WEDNESDAY)

Weights—the One-Set-per-Bodypart Workout

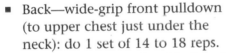

- Machine hack squat or Smith machine squat: do 1 set of 15 to 20 reps.

- Calves—the stair stepper will also be your calf workout, so just stretch each calf for 30 to 60 seconds. Be sure to keep your body erect and heels lowered as far as possible. Don't stop if you feel them burning; it is a good sign that you're really hitting the calves.
- Hamstrings and lower back—hyperextension: do 1 set of 10 to 13 reps.
- Chest—cable crossover: do 1 set of 10 to 13 reps.
- Shoulders and delts—standing bent-over dumbbell laterals: do 1 set of 12 to 14 reps.
- Back—seated cable row: do 1 set of 9 to 12 reps.
- Triceps—seated dumbbell French press: do 1 set of 10 to 14 reps.
- Biceps—thumbs-up cable curl with a rope: do 1 set of 16 to 22 reps.
- Abs—leg raise (hanging, machine, or lying down): do 1 set to failure.

For variety, try leg raises to tighten the lower abs.

For best results, allow the step to come all the way up and down.

Bring the knees up until the abs are at peak contraction. Experiment to find your peak point.

- Stretch: work all body groups with additional emphasis on any areas you want.

Cardio–Stair Stepper, 12 Minutes

- Place the balls of your feet on the end part of the steps.

- Keep your upper body erect—*no bending over!*
- Place your hands over the rails with a normal grip with your palms down. Do not use a reverse-grip (like too many people do) with your palms turned away from you.
- Use the "manual program."
- Begin stepping. Take full complete steps—no limited-motion quick-stepping stuff. Long-step strides is what you want.
- As you find your rhythm, loosen your grip on the rails until you can step without holding on to anything.
- Concentrate on taking long step strides and moving your arms back and forth and up and down until you are in the exercise groove.
- Allow each step to go all the way up so you feel the exercise working your glutes, hamstrings, and quads, and all the way down so you feel the big stretch and contraction in your calves. You'll find

this method to be an incredible calf shaper.

- Don't be concerned about speed. Go for full-step strides up and down and without stopping. Speed will come as you become better conditioned and used to doing this exercise.
- At the 12-minute mark, stop and get off. You're finished.
- Stretch: work all body groups with additional emphasis on any areas you want.

SAMPLE WORKOUT PLAN (FRIDAY)

Cardio–Stationary or Regular Bike, 12 minutes

- Elevate the seat so that when the pedal is down at the lowest position of the stroke, there's a slight bend to your knee.
- Begin pedaling and set the program for "manual training."

- Begin the program at level 2 and maintain 80 to 92 rpm for two minutes.
- At the two-minute mark, increase the level to 4 and maintain 80 to 85 rpm.
- At the five-minute mark, increase the level to 6 and maintain 80 rpm.
- At the eight-minute mark, decrease to level 3 and maintain 95 to 100 rpm.
- At the 10-minute mark, decrease the level to 2 and maintain 90 to 95 rpm.
- At the 11-minute mark, decrease the level to 1 and maintain 75 to 80 rpm.
- At the 12-minute mark, stop and get off. You're finished.

Weights–the One-Set-per-Bodypart Workout

- Leg press: do 1 set to failure, but pick a weight (not too heavy or light) so that you can do at least 15 reps.
- Calves—leg press toe raises: do 25 to 50 nonstop reps.

The benefits of looking and feeling great allow you to enjoy life in ways other people will never know.

Incline dumbbell flyes–pure chest magic!

To really make the triceps burn, keep your elbows above the torso.

- Stiff-legged deadlift (with barbell or dumbbells): do 1 set to failure, but pick a weight (not too heavy or light) so that you can do at least 15 reps.
- Chest—incline dumbbell flye: do 1 set of 10 to 13 reps.
- Shoulders/delts—standing dumbbell side lateral raise: do 1 set of 12 to 14 reps.
- Back—one-arm dumbbell row: do 1 set of 14 to 18 reps.
- Triceps—dumbbell kickback: do 1 set to failure (at least 10 reps) for each arm.
- Biceps—seated incline dumbbell curl (30- to 45-degree angle): do 1 set of 9 to 12 reps for each arm.
- Abs—trunk twist: continuous from side to side for two minutes.
- Stretch: work all body groups with additional emphasis on any areas you want.
- You're finished.

18

Workout 11: The Seven-Day Workout

Let me tell you a little bit about this workout. Some years ago when I began training, I had some friends who were serious about working out, came to the gym regularly, trained hard, ate right, got plenty of sleep, and got great results.

Yet, despite their best efforts and intentions, each of them still had a stubborn bodypart or two that always lagged behind the rest of the body. They tried using extra weights—nothing happened. They tried adding extra sets and reps—nothing happened. They even tried visualizing "biceps like mountains," as Arnold Schwarzenegger was so often quoted as saying. Still nothing. Finally, they hit on a workout that did it.

This workout was so different, so radical, and so "not the right way to train" that it worked. It worked so well that they told their friends, who told their friends, who told their friends, who told . . . well, you get the picture.

This workout will have you training the same bodypart and only the same bodypart every day for seven

days. It's intense. It'll shock that stubborn muscle like never before and give you results you may never have thought possible.

Here's how it works. Every 10 weeks, pick a bodypart that you would like to improve. Train that bodypart and no other every day for seven days. At the end of the seven days, take five days off from working that bodypart. After the rest period, resume training the bodypart using your regular routines.

So what workouts and exercises should you do? Well, since many of you have asked how to get better-looking arms, here is a great seven-day workout for biceps. Remember, you can apply these seven different types of workouts to *any* bodypart that's lagging. Simply pick the exercises for that bodypart that work best for your body, apply these workouts and rep schemes, and you'll get terrific results.

THE SEVEN-DAY BICEPS WORKOUT

Day 1: The 6/9 Compound Set with Barbell to Dumbbells

- After a warm-up of light barbell curls, pick a barbell heavy enough that you can curl for only 6 reps.
- With elbows close to your sides, curl the barbell with good strict form for 6 reps.
- Immediately put the barbell down and pick up two dumbbells heavy enough that you can curl for only 9 reps.
- Holding the dumbbells with a thumbs-up grip (palms facing each other), slowly curl the weights up and down until you've gotten a good stretch at the bottom of the movement and a good contraction at the top.
- After you complete 9 reps, set the weights down, rest less than 10

seconds, then go immediately back to the barbell and repeat.
- Do this for a total of 5 compound sets of 6 and 9 reps.
- After you've completed your fifth set, stop and stretch your biceps. Simply extend your arms down to your hips and turn your palms out and away from you. You should feel a good biceps stretch. Hold your arms in this stretched position for 30 to 60 seconds. After that, you're finished.

Day 2: The Heavy 3s Workout

This workout will use either barbells or dumbbells (your choice) and will use heavy weight and low reps.

- After a good warm-up of light-to-moderate-weight barbell curls, pick a heavy weight that you can curl only 3 times.
- You'll do these as standing curls, so don't cheat too much. A little (and I mean little) arch to the back or bend at the knees is OK, but not much. Make your biceps do the work.
- Concentrate on using good strict form; this will make the biceps work more intensely and give you better results.
- Here's how to do the reps. When you begin to curl the weight(s) up, make it an explosive, powerful movement—put a lot of force behind it.
- When you allow the weight(s) to come down, make sure you go twice as slow as when you curled the weight(s) up. If it takes two to three seconds to curl it up, take four to six seconds to lower it.
- Be sure to start and finish each rep with your arms fully extended at the bottom in order to give the biceps a great stretch.

- Do 5 sets of 3 reps.
- After you've completed your fifth set, stop and stretch your biceps.

Day 3: The 7-7-7 Workout

You choose either barbells or dumbbells for this workout. For variation, use something different from what you used for the Day 2 workout.

- You'll be working three ranges of the biceps curling arc with this workout: bottom to middle, middle to top, and bottom to top.
- Pick a weight(s) that's roughly about 50 to 60 percent of the heaviest 8-rep weight you can do. For example, if 60 pounds is the most you can dumbbell curl for 8 reps, then use about 30 pounds for this workout.
- Let's say you've decided to use dumbbells for this workout. Take those 30-pounders and sit on the edge of a flat bench.
- With your elbows close to your sides, curl both dumbbells up until they reach the halfway position.
- At the halfway position, lower the weights back down and repeat until you've done 7 reps.
- At the top of the seventh rep, curl the weights up until your biceps are fully contracted.
- Slowly lower the dumbbells down until they reach the halfway position, then curl them back up to the top.
- At the top of the seventh rep of the second part of this workout, lower the weights all the way to the starting position where your arms are fully extended and the biceps are fully stretched.
- Do the last seven reps as full-range reps curling the dumbbells all the way up and lowering them all the way down.

- The key to making this really effective is doing all 21 reps (7, 7, and 7) without any rest between reps. Talk about an incredible arm pump!
- Do 3 sets of 21 (7, 7, and 7) reps.
- After you've completed your third and final set, stop and stretch your biceps.

Day 4: The 83-Rep Workout

Time for a little change. This time you'll only do 1 set, but you'll do 83 nonstop reps. This little bit of insanity will pump more blood into those biceps than you've ever felt before. You'll especially feel the effects of this after three previous days of lower-rep and heavier-weight training.

- Use a barbell for this one. It's much easier, with less to think about, especially when you hit 50 or more reps!
- Choose a weight that's about 30 to 40 percent of the best weight you could use for 8 to 10 reps. For example, if the most you can barbell curl for 8 to 10 reps is 100 pounds, then use 30 to 40 pounds for this workout.
- You need to keep the weight moving and the biceps working. Even if the reps are slower, that's OK, just keep things moving.
- I suggest beginning with a nice controlled rhythm and keep that rhythm from rep 1 to rep 83.
- Breathe out when curling, and breathe in when lowering the weight.
- After you've completed the eighty-third rep, stop and stretch your biceps.

Day 5: The Limited-Range Reps Workout

Full-range reps are great and definitely have their place in training, but so do short, limited-range reps, especially when it comes to handling heavy weights. We'll make use of limited-range reps in this workout, and you can use them with any biceps exercise you like. We'll use them with preacher curls, something different to hit your biceps.

- Use the 45-degree (or so) angle side of the preacher bench.
- Grab an EZ-bar barbell with enough weight that you can full-range curl for only 1 to 2 reps.
- With the arm pad adjusted, grab the weight and curl it all the way up.
- Slowly lower the weight about three to five inches and stop. Then curl it back up until your biceps are fully contracted.
- Do this for 9 more reps for a total of 10 limited-range reps.
- Rack the weight and rest one to two minutes before doing your next set.
- If you could easily do 10 reps with that weight, increase the weight by 15 percent and do another 10 limited-range reps.
- As long as the weights are fairly easy to curl for 10 reps, keep increasing the weight until you find the amount that makes you and your biceps work. That's the key; getting great results means making your muscles work.
- Do a total of 4 sets of 10 limited-range reps.
- After you've completed your fourth set, stop and stretch your biceps.

Day 6: The Static-Hold Workout

This is a great workout to use a barbell and I'm going to tell you a little trick that will make it easier to do, yet harder at the same time. You'll do a standing barbell curl, but I want you to

place your upper back against a wall to prevent you from cheating.

- Grab a barbell with a weight that's about 70 to 80 percent of what you would use if you were doing your best barbell curls for 6 to 8 reps. For example, if that weight is usually 100 pounds, then use 70 to 80 pounds for this workout.
- With your upper back against the wall and elbows close to your body, curl the weight up, stop halfway, and hold the weight in that position.
- Hold it there for 10 to 15 seconds; slowly lower it; count one, two, three; curl it back up to the halfway point; and hold it again for another 10 to 15 seconds.
- Do this eight more times for a total of 10 static-hold reps.
- After the first set of 10 reps, put the weight down, stretch your biceps (like you've done at the end

When used correctly, big weights produce big results.

of all the previous workouts), and rest one to two minutes.

- Do another set of 10 static-hold reps and stretch again.
- Do a total of 4 sets of 10 static-hold reps.
- After you've completed your fourth set, stop and stretch your biceps.

Day 7: The 3 × 10-30-60 Workout

I think I've saved the best for last. For this workout, you'll do three biceps exercises back-to-back, but each one with a different rep pattern and purpose.

- The first exercise is seated alternating (one arm, then the next) dumbbell curls for 10 reps. Pick a weight heavy enough for you to do 10 tough reps with good form.
- Sit on the end of a bench, keep your upper body erect and elbows close to your sides, and curl the left arm up first until the biceps are fully contracted. Then as you lower the left arm, bring the right arm up and do the same.
- Do this for 10 reps.
- Immediately after the tenth rep, put the weights down and go to a machine preacher curl and begin curling it for a total of 30 reps.
- Be sure to lower the arm bar all the way down and then bring it up only far enough until the biceps are fully flexed and contracted. Don't bring it back too far to where the stress is taken off the biceps, which can easily happen if you're not careful.
- Lower the bar and repeat. Be sure to also keep a good steady rhythm going, just like a machine.

- After the thirtieth rep, immediately move to the third and final exercise, the kneeling cable curl with a straight bar.
- Use a weight that's about 50 percent of what you normally use for a straight set of 8 to 10 reps. Again, if that weight is typically 100 pounds, use about 50 pounds for this last exercise.
- With the straight bar connected to a cable in both hands, keep your upper torso erect and squat down in front of the weight stack.
- Place the outside of your arms on the inside of your thighs (inner thighs).
- Allow your arms to fully stretch and extend. Then curl the weight up and back toward your shoulders until your biceps are fully contracted.
- Lower the weight back down and repeat.
- Do 60 nonstop reps.
- Keep the weight and reps going until you reach 60—don't stop in between. This is the last exercise of the set, and this one is the clincher.
- After the sixtieth rep, stretch your biceps for one minute, take another minute to rest with no stretch, and then do one more set of the same three exercises with the same reps.
- After your second set of 10, 30, and 60, stop and stretch your biceps.

Remember, at the end of the seven days, take five days off from working that bodypart. After the rest period, resume training the bodypart using your regular routines.

19

Workout 12: The Instinctive Workout

I like this workout because it truly is a lot of fun. The previous workouts are fun, too. OK, the heavy-weight kind of training isn't exactly the easiest thing in the world to do, but you must admit, it does get results.

This workout will teach you to think and get in touch with your body like you never have before. I'm amazed at just how many people will train for months and years at a time and still never really know what kinds of workouts, exercises, sets, and reps their bodies respond best to. Any wonder why they still look and feel the same year after year?

The workout is called instinctive because each workout will be different and will be determined by you when you're in the gym and ready to work out. How many times have you thought that tomorrow you would train such and such bodypart and use such and such weights and reps, only to find that once tomorrow came, you didn't have the energy you had the day before, or you really didn't feel like working those bodyparts anymore?

Yet, if you listened to all those who say, "Instinctive training is hogwash" or "You've got to have a plan and if you're not training heavy (light, brief, with short-range reps, long-range reps), and your strength is not going up or whatever, then all you're doing is ineffective training and wasting your time," then you've closed your mind to possibilities that may work for you. Listening to such talk makes me wonder, are you some kind of machine whose job is simply to lift weights in some predetermined way? And, unless you are getting a certain type of result, are you not getting any benefits or having any fun? Baloney.

You don't have to lift heavy weights or get stronger to enjoy working out. You don't have to use only short-range or long-range reps to get great results. If you like working out because it makes your mind and body feel good, then that's all that matters. So forget about listening to what all the others say. Let them do what they believe will give them a good, enjoyable workout. Working out isn't a competition. It's what you want it to be, period.

So what will your instinctive workout be like? That's for you to design. Here, however, are some suggestions that you might like.

- Don't preplan any exercises until you're actually in the gym and ready to work out. If, after you've chosen and begun the exercises, you're not feeling your muscle pump, stop and immediately try a different exercise for that same bodypart, one that you can feel.
- Do 2 to 3 sets per bodypart. That means you'll do two different exercises for that bodypart—perhaps a barbell or dumbbell exercise followed with a machine-type of movement.
- Experiment with a combination of reps while training each bodypart. For example, when training your chest, you might try dumbbell incline presses with heavier weights for 5 to 8 reps and then use lighter weights on the pec deck or flat bench flyes for 20 to 30 nonstop reps.
- During this workout, practice closing your eyes while doing some of the exercises (I suggest you keep them wide open during any exercise that uses heavy weight) in order to close off some of the distractions you would normally notice when they're open. This will help you make the mind-muscle connection and increase concentration on making the muscle work and actually feeling the nuance of each rep. So many people who train are like mindless machines whose goal is to lift a certain amount of weight a certain number of times and that's it. Yet all the while, they're missing out on what a great rep feels like. *Great reps mean great sets,*

which mean great workouts, which mean great results. Keep that "in mind."

- Have a great variety of exercises you like to do that you've found actually work well for your body. Book and magazines are filled with great pictures of models doing all kinds of cool-looking exercises, but whether or not those exercises may be best for you is another thing entirely.

As you learned earlier in this book, take the time (don't worry, it won't take long) to find the best three to five exercises for each bodypart that really work well for you, and choose from them each and every workout. Your body gets bored very quickly, so if you give it something new and different all the time in new and different ways, it will really increase your inter-

Change your workouts each time, and do what your body needs for *that* workout.

est and motivation to keep working out, not to mention keep your body off-guard and responding well to all the new training stimuli.

- Another great instinctive training tool is to make it a little contest with yourself to pick one exercise and set your personal best, even if it means only doing 1 more rep than you did before. This is important because your mind remembers something called "the last deposit." This means that if the best you've ever done on the lat pulldowns was 11 reps with 160 pounds, your mind amazingly reminds you that 11 reps with that weight was your best. So doing that extra twelfth rep not only breaks that old last-deposit memory, but more important for your success, gives you powerful positive feedback that helps propel you to even greater future success.

  Remember, you don't have to break a major record to get these amazing mental benefits. The littlest things can produce great results, because the mind doesn't care if you lifted an extra two pounds or two hundred pounds; it only remembers you did better than you've done before.

- By all means, do a workout, exercise, set, or rep unlike you would normally do or have done in the past. Experiment, get creative, and go out on a limb and try something radically different. The key here is to break the habit patterns we so easily get into by doing the same types of workouts and exercises in the same sorts of ways. Boring, boring, boring.

  Use a combination of all the workouts and exercises you learn in this book, and put them together in combinations you think might be pretty cool to try. Whatever it is, if you can dream it and think it, then do it because it's right for you. Don't tell anyone what you're doing and why. Just do it and see what happens. Experimentation has been behind every great achievement in life, and creating a great workout that's just right for you is no different. Create, create, create!

Here are only three of the unlimited kinds of the great instinctive workout that works the whole body in one workout.

INSTINCTIVE WORKOUT #1

Chest

Cable Crossover to Wide-Arm Push-Up Do 9 reps on the cable crossover, immediately followed by wide-arm push-ups (with feet elevated on a flat bench) for as many reps as possible. Do 2 sets of back-to-back exercises with less than 15 seconds of rest between sets.

The farther apart your arms are, the more you'll feel it in the chest.

Back

Reverse-Grip Lat Pulldown with Straight Bar
Do 2 sets of 15 to 18 reps. Rest no longer than 25 seconds between sets.

Shoulders

Heavy Dumbbell Side Raise Only raise the dumbbells three inches from your sides and do not let them come down and touch your sides. Do 6 to 9 reps, immediately followed by light dumbbell side laterals for 13 to 17 nonstop reps. Do 2 sets with no more than 20 seconds of rest between sets.

Triceps

Seated Dumbbell French Press Do 2 sets of 40 reps. Be sure to get a complete stretch and full extension from top to bottom of the movement. Rest no longer than 15 seconds between sets.

Biceps

Dumbbell Concentration Curl (Seated or Standing Bent Over) Do 11 reps for each arm, immediately followed by standing barbell curls for 25 nonstop reps. Rest no longer than 10 seconds between sets. Do 2 sets.

Hamstrings and Quads

Lying Leg Curl Do 30 reps, immediately followed by leg extensions for 30 reps. Do 2 nonstop back-to-back sets with only enough rest to quickly move from one machine to the next.

Calves

Standing Toe Raise (Balls of Feet on the Edge of an Elevated Platform) Do 1 set of 100 nonstop reps. Vary the range of motion from full-range at the beginning to short-range reps as you near the end of the 100 reps. In fact, that's all

Allow the arm to completely stretch at the bottom of the exercise.

Bring the weight up until you feel a peak contraction—any higher reduces intensity.

you'll be able to do once your calves hit 100 reps. What a burn and what a great results-producer!

Abs

Bicycle Crunches Keep your body flat, head and neck up off the floor, knees bent, and legs moving in a circular motion and back toward your upper body each time you crunch. Do 2 sets of 50 reps, and rest no more than 10 seconds between sets.

Stretch

Take 10 to 20 seconds to lightly stretch each bodypart worked, before leaving. Great job!

INSTINCTIVE WORKOUT #2

Shoulders

Bent-Over Opposing-Grip Cable Laterals Do 1 set of at least 30 continuous reps. Start off with the upper torso bent over at 90 degrees. Then, as you continue to do sets, start elevating your upper torso until it reaches the near-vertical position. You'll feel this exercise all over your delts, and you'll also find just the right spots where you'll feel it most.

Chest

Close-Hand Push-Ups (Feet Elevated on Flat Bench) Place your hands together (one on top of the other) and position them just under the lower chest area. Place your feet on an elevated flat bench behind you. The higher your feet are off the ground, the more resistance and the harder the movement will be. Lower your body until it rests on top of your hands, then press up and lock your elbows. Repeat for 1 set of as many reps as possible.

Triceps

Reverse-Grip Pressdown with Straight Bar Your triceps will be smoking from the push-ups and this movement will really finish them off. Take a straight bar and

Keep the upper body in the same position throughout.

Straighten the arms and raise the cables high enough so that you feel the burn in the rear delts.

do pressdowns like you would normally do them, but use an underhand grip. Do 1 set of 25 reps.

Back

Seated Cable Row Use a stirrup-style bar where both palms face each other. Keep a slight bend at the knees and your upper torso erect. Pull your elbows back behind you and the bar down low and back until it hits your lower stomach. Lower the weight, fully extend your arms in front of you, and allow your upper torso to come only slightly forward for a good lat stretch. Do 1 set of 12 to 15 reps.

Biceps

Seated Dumbbell Incline Curl Adjust the bench so that it's at a 30- to 45-degree angle. Keep your upper body securely positioned throughout the exercise and only allow your shoulders to come slightly forward, if at all. Keep your

Try trunk twists with a broomstick and include seated knee-ups every other workout.

elbows pulled in close to the sides of the bench, and turn your arms slightly outward and away from your body. Do 1 set of 11 to 14 reps. Be sure to allow the weights to come all the way down so your arms are fully locked out, and all the way up until your biceps reach full contraction.

Calves

Seated Calf Raise Pick a weight that will allow you to do 25 to 45 reps. Place the balls of your feet on the end of the foot platform, and place the upper leg pad just right above the upper knee area. Lower your heels until they reach maximal stretch; then raise your heels until your calves are maximally contracted. Slowly lower and repeat for 1 set of 25 to 45 reps. Stretch your calves (see instinctive workout 1).

Hamstrings

Stiff-Legged Dumbbell Deadlift Take two dumbbells and keep them close to your sides. With a slight bend at the knees, allow your upper body to bend over. As you do, lower the dumbbells down until they reach your shin and ankle level. Keep your head up and looking forward from start to finish. Feel the exercise stretch your hamstrings (leg biceps). You'll feel it more intensely if you keep the weights close to your body throughout the exercise. Do 1 set of 12 to 20 reps.

Quads

Front Squat (Heels Elevated) Warm up by doing 1 set of 20 to 25 brisk knee bends. After the warm-up, place a barbell across your shoulders/upper chest/clavicle area. Position your heels on either a one-inch wood block or two 25-pound plates (one heel on each plate). Just like in a regular back squat, allow your knees to bend and your

Front squats are among the most effective exercises you can do.

upper body to come down until your upper legs are at about the parallel position. Keep your upper body erect, and your head up and looking forward. Do 20 nonstop reps. Remember, just like a machine: up, down, up, down, and no rest between reps.

Abs

Trunk Twists with Broomstick You can do these either seated or standing. Place a broomstick behind your neck and with your hands gripping both ends, begin twisting from side to side. Start off by doing slow, limited-range-of-motion twists, and increase the tempo and range of motion after one to two minutes of twisting. Do three to five minutes of continuous trunk twists.

Stretch

Take 10 to 20 seconds and lightly stretch each bodypart worked. Great job!

INSTINCTIVE WORKOUT #3

This workout will use heavier weights for 3 sets of lower reps (unless otherwise noted), with rest breaks of 45 to 70 seconds between sets (unless otherwise noted), and rest breaks between bodyparts of no more than 90 seconds. Always remember, whether you're doing 1 set or 3 sets, low reps or high reps, intensity is the name of the game for results. Think of how you can make your muscles work harder (not just by using heavier weights) in the same, if not shorter, period of time.

Hyper-Bench Leg Curl

This exercise will take care of not only your hamstrings, but your lower back and glutes as well. Be sure to position your body so that your upper body is forward enough and off the bench that you're able to use a full range of movement. Allow only the upper body to move by bending only at the waist. Lower your upper torso until you get a good stretch and then raise it until it is parallel and in a straight line with your legs. Really contract the lower back, hamstrings, and glutes at the top of the exercise. Do 3 sets of 6 reps.

Leg Press to Toe Raise

This is another exercise that you'll use to work more than one muscle group—in this case, quads and calves. You can use a vertical, 45-degree, or 30-degree leg press. With feet placed high on the foot platform, position them so that they are about 12 inches apart and the toes are turned slightly outward. Bend your knees and lower the platform until your glutes are almost ready to come up and out of the seated starting position. This should mean your upper thighs will be roughly straight up and down and almost in the vertical 90-degree position. Do 6 to 8 reps.

After the eighth rep, rack the weight. Quickly change feet position so that the balls of your feet are now placed at the bottom of the foot platform. With the rack secured and racked, allow your ankles to bend and the platform to come down as far as possible until you are getting a great stretch in your calves. Your knees should at most only have a slight bend to them. If you're doing it right, you will feel this stretch in your calves and up higher back behind the knees near the lower insertion point of the hamstrings. Do 20 to 25 nonstop reps. After this toe raise set, rest only 10 to 15 seconds and do another set of leg presses, and repeat. Do a total of 3 back-to-back sets.

Hanging Knee Raise

This is a great exercise for the lower abs. With your hands about shoulder-width apart, take an overhand grip on a chinning bar that's positioned high enough so you can hang from it with

When doing hanging knee raises, do a few reps with legs straight in front and a few to the sides.

your entire body stretched and your feet not touching the ground. Keeping your upper torso erect, raise your upper legs so that your knees come up and toward your stomach area. Really make the abdominals contract as your legs come up and your lower torso slightly bends forward and upward. Think of it as a U-shape. Lower and repeat. Do 3 sets to your limit.

Dumbbell Incline Flye

You'll like this nice chest movement. I suggest using a bench you can elevate to about 25 to 40 degrees. Do these like regular flat bench dumbbell flyes (think of it like putting your arms around a big wide barrel), only inclined and elevated. Get a nice, deep stretch at the bottom. As you bring the weights up in a semicircle, don't let them touch each other at the top of the exercise. Keep them about six to eight inches apart to keep a good contraction on the pecs. Do 3 sets of 6 to 10 reps.

Barbell Front Press

Go ahead and do this one standing. Take a barbell and use a wider-than-shoulder-width grip. Start with the barbell resting on the front deltoids. Press the weight straight up and overhead until your arms are fully locked out. Lower the weight to the starting position and repeat. Do 3 sets of 9 to 12 reps. As a real burner, try stopping the weight about halfway and then press it up about three to four inches. Do this for about 10 real quick delt burns.

Dumbbell Kickback

A great triceps movement. You can either use two dumbbells at once or one arm at a time. The most important thing to remember is keep a slight bend to the knees. Have your upper torso bent over at 70 to 90 degrees, keep your upper arm locked tight into your side, and make sure your elbow is raised higher than your back. Extend the arm(s) with the dumbbell(s) up and behind you until your elbow is locked out, hold in the contracted position for a second or two, and then slowly return to the starting position. Do 3 sets of your limit.

Reverse-Grip EZ-Bar or Barbell Row

You can do these with a barbell or EZ-bar. Try both and see which feels more comfortable to do. For the EZ-bar, grab the EZ-bar with a reverse-grip (under-hand grip), and place your upper body in a 60- to 80-degree position. Keeping your head up and looking forward, bring the weight up and into your waist and your elbows behind you. In this position, really contract the lats. The farther back you can bring your elbows behind you, the more you'll be able to feel it in your back and lat muscles. Lower the bar and repeat. Do 3 sets of 5 to 7 reps.

Bent-Over Barbell Concentration Curl

This will really get the blood flowing in those arms, especially after 3 sets of reverse-grip EZ-bar rows. Take a barbell, and with your legs straight, allow your upper torso to bend over until it's at about 90 degrees or parallel to the floor. While holding the barbell, let your arms hang down until they are completely straight up and down. Keeping your upper arms in that position, curl the weight up until your biceps are fully contracted. Don't allow the weight to come back toward you any farther than that. You want to keep the biceps stretched at the bottom and contracted at the top. Do 3 sets of 20 to 30 nonstop reps. Allow no more than 20 seconds of rest between sets.

Stretch

Take 10 to 20 seconds and lightly stretch each bodypart worked, before leaving. Great job!

The reverse grip allows the arms to come back farther for a better back contraction.

Whether you choose a barbell or a dumbbell, always keep the upper arm stationary and use nonstop reps.

20

Workout 13: The One-Set Workout

Don't you wish you had more hours in a day? I think we all do. Look at your life and all the things that beg for a precious piece of your time. Talk about doing a juggling act!

What if I told you I've got an ideal workout for you if you have little time or simply don't want a multiple set bodypart workout? You can even use this to throw in a bit of cross-training.

Still thinking about it? OK, what if I told you that this workout takes much less time but will offer nearly the same benefits as a multiple-set routine? Sound too good to be true? But it is the truth.

ONE SET, BABY, JUST ONE SET!

I'm talking one set here, but to make this workout a real workout, we need to make sure you're creating enough horsepower (i.e., intensity) to strengthen and tone your muscles. That means you'll lift heavier weights but use far fewer sets than conventional multiple-set training.

That's the first part. The second is, after you've intensely worked a muscle, you've got to give it enough rest so it can recuperate and get stronger. Here's an alarming fact: Most people are frustrated with their strength-training workouts because they are overtrained in sets and reps and undertrained in workout intensity. Always remember, *it's not how long you work out that counts. It's what you do and how effectively you work out when you're there.* Remember what I've told you about intensity? Bingo. That's just what I'm talking about here.

CAN ONE-SET TRAINING REALLY WORK?

Over the years, numerous studies have proven the effectiveness of one-set training. Noted exercise researcher, lecturer, and author Wayne Wescott, Ph.D., research and fitness director at South Shore YMCA in Quincy, Massachusetts, shares his findings.

Most people just don't have a lot of time to train, and they want an effective workout that will fit into a relatively brief time span. For many, the warm-up, cool-down, flexibility, cardiovascular, and strength training take up to an hour, which they'll usually try to fit in three times a week.

Thousands of our members use one-set training consisting of 12 different exercises. The beauty of this is that it takes them only about 90 seconds to do each set so the total strength-training workout for the entire body takes only 20 to 30 minutes.

For years our studies have shown that the average beginner on one-set training adds about three pounds of lean tissue and increases his or her strength by 60 percent in just eight weeks. In all honesty, I don't know if you can add much more than that doing triple and quadruple sets.

A one set versus multiple set study was done by Mike Pollock, Ph.D., at the University of Florida Medical School. The results were presented at an ACSM (American College of Sports Medicine) conference and published in Medicine & Science in Sports & Exercise.

The study, which tested leg extension and leg curl strength, found exactly the same strength gain between the one-set group and the three-set group.

We did a study of one-set versus two-set versus three-set training that used chin-ups and dips. We, too, found statistically identical improvements.

The bottom line is one set works well and it's practical. We've found that 95 percent of the people on one-set training like it so much, they stay with it. That's impressive!

DON'T RUSH A GOOD THING

Here's something important to remember, and it's something not widely talked about. *Slow down.* The good news is you don't have to rush from set to set to get the vast majority of physical, neuromuscular, metabolic, and performance benefits that go along with high-intensity circuit weight training.

One of the highly respected names in the fitness research business is James E. Wright, Ph.D. Dr. Wright, along with colleagues from the U.S. Army Research Institute of Environmental Medicine (and published in *Medicine & Science in Sports & Exercise*), conducted a study of one-set training at the U.S. Military Academy. They found that over the course of a 10-week training program, whether the rest period was 15 seconds, one minute, or two minutes made surprisingly little difference in the amount of strength gained, improvement in aerobic or anaerobic capacity, or body composition.

But the one important thing that was drawn from this research was that putting maximum effort into each and every set was more important in terms of results than moving faster—rushing—from set to set.

Now let me tell you, 15- to 30-second rest periods between sets are extremely demanding, mentally as well as physically. Is it any surprise that such training is considered by many, many experts who know their stuff in this field as among the most demanding type of training there is? Not surprisingly, it's probably one of the primary causes of individuals quitting. It is simply too much for most people to work out two to three times per week and give everything they've got for 15 to 20 continuous minutes. Talk about being too much like work. Yikes!

If I could, I would tell a thousand different ways to make highly effective, high-intensity training simple, quick, and easy. But, there really aren't any such ways. OK, I will make it a bit easier. If you just increase the rest period between sets up to two minutes, that alone will keep you from burning out.

However, as you become better conditioned, which I promise you will, start reducing your rest period by 30 seconds every two weeks so you'll have a conditioning goal to continually shoot for. You'll find this to be really important and a real kick for your training success.

The big goal here is for you to simply make exercise a part of your life. You don't need to set any records—unless, of course, you want to—nor make exercise some kind of punishment. What fun is that? Just start doing a little one-set training whenever you feel like it and you'll get great results.

THE WARM-UP

I suggest doing your cardio training before your one-set workout. The reason? Your body needs to be warmed up, and getting on the bike, stair stepper, or treadmill for 10 to 25 minutes before you train is a great way to get the blood flowing and the muscles working. (Most people who 1-set train don't have much time, so that's why we've reduced the cardio workout time.) After cardio, do a few no-weight exercises like good mornings, knee bends, arm circles, or knee raises along with 10 to 30 seconds of static stretches for each muscle group. This should take about 5 to 10 minutes at max. After that, you're ready.

HOW TO START

Many people like to always begin and end their workouts in a certain way, working the various muscle groups in a particular order. That's all well and good if that's what you must do, but I say do something different every time you work out. Working out can be a tough thing to do, even when you're highly motivated, and to always work out in the same way is a quick way for you to become bored and unenthused—

a real drainer for your workout motivation.

Think about it. Don't you like to do something different, to be a bit surprised and to look forward to doing something new? Variety is the spice of life, and the way you can spice up your workouts and results is to keep your body off-guard and out of the training rut by beginning and ending your workouts with different exercises.

What should you do? As you learned earlier in the book, always begin and end your workouts working different muscle groups. One day start with the chest. The next workout end with the chest or put it in the middle of the workout. Mix things up all the time.

Next, for each bodypart you're working, pick any one of the three to five exercises you've found that work best for you and your body. These are "your" exercises, and because these work best for you, use them.

HOW TO PROGRESS

One of the big keys to progress is what you have just learned: to always do something different whenever you train. The next big key is workout intensity: to make your workouts more intense during the same or less amount of time you normally take to train.

Another big factor to progressing is to not train too often. What, am I nuts? Relax, let me explain. So many people are overtrained from working out too much too often, and they are confused about why they aren't progressing. They look and feel the same month after month, year after year. Overtraining is one of the biggest reasons why.

Even doing too much 1-set training too often will burn you out. You're not some kind of robot or machine that can train all the time and be expected to always get great results. For goodness' sake, you're human, and though your body needs exercise, it also needs rest.

One of the best ways I've found to prevent workout burnout is to take forced rest breaks. And the time to take them is when you're making your best progress. That's right. Most people will only take a break from training either when they are so burned out that they're no longer making any progress or when they get sick or injured. But that's when their bodies are telling them, "Hey, listen here, pal, I've been trying to get your attention all these weeks, months, and years, and you think you know your body better than me, your body? Well, you don't, and to show you and make you stop your goofiness, here's an injury or sickness or burnout to finally get your attention." Sounds a bit far-fetched perhaps, but that's essentially what happens when you don't give your body the rest it needs when it needs it. So here's how to do just that.

For every four to six weeks of consistent training, take one complete week off. That means no training, just rest. I don't care if your training is at the best it has ever been and you're ready to set a new Olympic record. Take the time off. By taking these forced rest breaks, you end a workout cycle when your body is climbing the upward peak. Resting while it's climbing this peak sets the starting point for your next four- to six-week cycle of training.

I've found four to six weeks to be optimal because it allows the body to be trained with high intensity but doesn't work it so hard for so long that it cannot quickly recover from the training period. This is what you want because it essentially allows you to stay very motivated about your training and gives you great results year-round, not to mention that it greatly minimizes injury. In fact, in the 20-plus years I've

been training, I've never had an injury. It's because I've made what I've just taught you one of the cornerstones of my training program. Do it and you'll see exactly what I mean.

THE BEST TRAINING TIPS

The best tips are only those that work for you. Everyone who trains has his or her own ideas about the perfect exercise, food plan, or program, but none of that means beans if they don't work for you. Read all that you want, listen to well-meaning people, ask a boatload of questions, and then start applying what you've seen, heard, and read to your training. If you like it and it works for you, keep it. If it doesn't, don't hesitate to throw it out and find something else that will work.

Come up with a program, exercises, and variations that make working out fun for you. Be unlike all the others and create your own signature program that only you do. Some years ago, I saw a guy riding a stationary bike that was placed near a lat pulldown machine. While he was riding the bike doing his cardio training, he would do lat pulldowns with a light weight for 10 to 15 minutes. He told me it really conditioned him for endurance sports. It was the strangest looking exercise I had ever seen, but it worked for him and that was all that mattered.

So many folks are afraid of doing something different because of what other people will say and think. Who really cares? Other people are not devoting time out of *your* life to work *your* body. They're doing their thing and, friend, you do yours.

I will give you a few basic training tips that will work for anyone. Keep your workouts brief, intense, always new and different, and most of all, a lot of fun and something you really look forward to doing.

THE ONE-SET WORKOUT

- Front legs (quads)
  Leg extension, 2 warm-up sets
- Back legs (quads and hamstrings)
  Leg extension compound-setted (i.e., doing two exercises for the same bodypart) to sissy squat, 1 set to failure
     Leg curl (any variation), 1 set to failure
- Calves
  Standing calf raise (machine or freestanding), 1 set to failure
- Chest
  Dumbbell flat bench or incline bench press, 1 set to failure
- Back
  Reverse-grip front pulldown, 1 set to failure

- Shoulders
  Dumbbell side lateral, 1 set to failure
- Biceps
  Seated dumbbell alternating curl, 1 set to failure
- Triceps
  Reverse-grip triceps pressdown, 1 set to failure
- Abdominals
  Crunch (arms across chest), 1 set to failure
     Hanging leg raise, 1 set to failure
     Seated leg raise, 1 set to failure
- Stretch
  Stretch your whole body after you've finished training a bodypart and again after you've finished training all your bodyparts.

Try the reverse-grip front pulldown with either the triangle bar or the straight bar.

21

Workout 14: The Balance Workout

This is an excellent workout because it teaches your body to become balanced—stronger in areas where you may be weak. Enough can't be said for finding balance in all areas of life. Many of us are either too much of this or too little of that, all the while never centering ourselves with just the right balance that can bring us the greatest sense of inner peace, joy, and fulfillment.

The same is true for your workouts. You need a good balance between resistance and cardio training, heavy weights and lighter weights, full-range reps and short-range reps, one set and multiple sets, and of course, using different workouts to keep you looking forward to working out month after month and year after year.

I'm surprised at just how many people who have been working out for years haven't developed the proper balance, not only in how their bodies look, but more important, in how they function. It's amazing to see how many of these people—who have trained long and hard for years and are capable of lifting some amazing poundages—have so much trouble handling much lighter weights when asked to do them in different ways.

This can be a real detriment, because an important thing to gain from all the hours of training is to be able to apply the hard work and results in the gym to the "real world" outside of the gym, for any sport or activity one wants to do. This workout will help you do just that.

You are going to use your stabilizer muscles and get out of the fixed positions of working out. You will build balance, supportive tissue strength, endurance, and capability. It may seem a little strange at first, but stay with me, for it'll all be worthwhile once you see and feel the results.

LEGS UP AND OFF THE FLOOR

This is a great way to eliminate the cheating that you see so many people do when they do bench presses, lat pulldowns, shoulder presses, and any other upper-body exercise that uses the legs for support. By taking the feet and legs out of the picture, you must rely on your upper-body muscles—those bigger main muscles you're wanting to work and those smaller stabilizer muscles you don't even think about working—to help you do each exercise. This not only forces you to use ideal form in order to complete each rep and exercise, but makes your muscles work harder because you've taken away their help to cheat—the legs.

You'll be amazed at just how fast your body will kick in those other stabilizer muscles to help you do each rep and exercise once you take the legs out of the equation. And you'll be equally amazed at how fast you'll find *your* right exercise groove after a few sets of no-leg-help training.

Don't freak out if you have to use considerably lighter weight than you've been used to. This is a different way to train and you'll find it to be quite intense—even with the lighter weight—

once you take the legs out of the way. Here are some great legs-up exercises and tips that'll help.

CHEST

Dumbbell Bench Press (Incline, Decline, and Flat)

If you do these on a flat bench, bring your legs up and bend your knees, and keep them there throughout the exercise. If you do these on an incline, bring your legs up and off the ground and rest your feet in front of you on a small platform. For decline, just keep your feet off the floor.

Dumbbell Flye (Incline and Flat)

If you do these on a flat bench, bring your legs up and bend your knees, and keep them there throughout the exercise. If you do these on an incline, bring your legs up and in close to your

Keeping the feet up and off the floor is a great way to increase balance, focus on form, and use muscles you don't use every day.

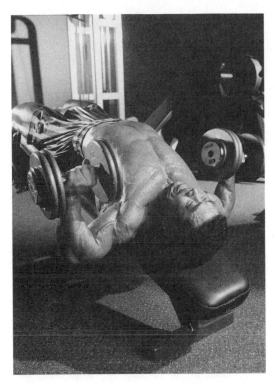

Decline flyes can give your chest and overall physique the balance it needs.

body, and place your feet below your glutes on the bench.

Barbell Bench Press (Flat)

If you do these on a flat bench, bring your legs up and bend your knees, and keep them there throughout the exercise.

Pec Deck

There are a couple of different leg positions. One is to bring your legs up and elevate them high enough so that your feet are in front of you at about waist level. This minimizes the amount of help your legs will be able to give and throws the emphasis of the exercise to the upper torso, where you want it. The other is to lock your feet behind you either on the seat support or with only the tops of your toes touching the ground. The whole point is to take your legs and feet out of the exercise so that your upper torso does the work.

BACK

Lat Pulldown (Reverse-Grip, Overhand Grip, Front, and Rear)

Do these just like normal pulldowns, only let your knees come straight down so that they're in a straight line with your upper body and place your feet behind you. Again, make sure only the tops of your toes touch the floor in order to minimize any help your legs can give you. You want your upper body to do the work, not your legs.

Chin-Up

This is probably the best no-leg back exercise, simply because it uses your bodyweight and forces you to use all those upper-body muscles you need to pull your body up. Don't worry if you can only do a rep or two at first. Simply do your chin-up rep(s) first, then finish your set with lat pulldowns in the way just described. When doing chin-ups, be sure to keep your legs bent and behind your body, and your upper body straight up and down.

SHOULDERS

Seated Barbell or Dumbbell Press

You probably think the seated barbell or dumbbell press is impossible to do without keeping your legs firmly on the floor, but it's not. There are two ways to do this exercise.

One way is to elevate your feet in front of you and allow them to rest on a bench or platform so they are high enough—about one to two feet off the ground. This way your legs will only help drive your lower body tighter into the seat to support you. This is different from keeping your feet on the ground, which flexes your legs and

Use lighter weights for this one.

The goal of doing the excerise this way is to minimize "the cheat" and maximize the focus.

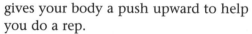

gives your body a push upward to help you do a rep.

The other way is to keep your feet behind you and knees straight down, just like you did on the lat pulldowns. You've got to find a bench high enough to allow this, but this is also a great way to minimize your feet and maximize working your delts.

Seated Dumbbell Lateral Raise

Do these with your legs and feet completely extended and straight out in front so only your heels touch the floor. This position will work for front, rear, and side dumbbell raises.

Seated Dumbbell Shrug

Position your feet out in front of you just the way you did on the seated dumbbell laterals. Keep your upper torso erect, and with a dumbbell in each hand hanging straight down at your sides and close to the bench,

shrug your shoulders straight up and down. Be sure to raise those shoulders up as high as you can and hold them there for one to two seconds, then slowly lower your shoulders and the weights down until you get a full stretch.

TRICEPS

Lying EZ-Bar French Press

If you do these on a flat bench, bring your legs up and bend your knees to about waist level, and keep them there throughout the exercise. The upper body should stay stationary in one position; your arms are the only muscle group that should move.

Seated Dumbbell French Press (One-Arm and Two-Arm) Overhead

Use the same kind of feet and leg position that you used for the seated barbell or dumbbell press. One way is to elevate your feet in front of you and allow them to rest on a bench or platform so they are high enough—about one to two feet off the ground. This way your legs will only help drive your lower body tighter into the seat to support you. This is different from keeping your feet on the ground, which flexes your legs and gives your body a push upward to help you do a rep.

The other way is to keep your feet behind you and knees straight down, just like you did on the lat pulldowns. You've got to find a bench high enough to allow this, but this is also a great way to minimize your feet and maximize working only your upper torso.

Lying French Press with Low-Pulley Machine

This exercise will be very similar to a lying EZ-bar French press; however, instead of using a barbell, you'll use either a rope, curved bar, or straight bar that's connected to a cable low-pulley weight stack machine.

You'll use a flat bench, and you need to bring your legs up and bend your knees to about waist level, and keep them there throughout the exercise. The upper body should stay stationary in one position; your arms are the only muscle group that should move.

BICEPS

Seated Dumbbell Incline Curl

There are a couple of different leg positions. One is to bring your legs up and elevate them high enough so that they are in front of you at about waist level. This minimizes the amount of help your legs will be able to give and throws the emphasis of the exercise to the upper torso, where you want it. The

other is to lock your feet behind you either on the seat support or with only the tops of your toes touching the ground. The whole point is to take your legs and feet out of the exercise so that your upper torso does the work.

Either way you choose, be sure that you keep your elbows positioned close to the bench and near your body, and your arms turned out to your sides and away from your body. Keep them in this position throughout the exercise. You'll find this will help minimize cheating and will isolate the biceps more.

Get a good stretch at the beginning of your exercise.

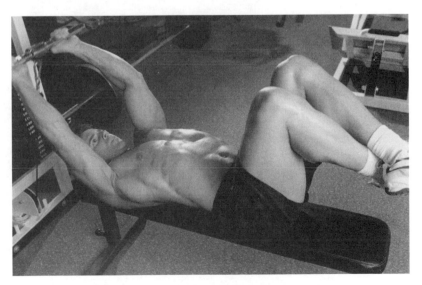

Be sure to keep the cable traveling in the same plane of movement.

Flat Bench Lying Dumbbell Curl (Elbows In and Arms Out)

If you do these on a flat bench, bring your legs up and bend your knees to about waist level, and keep them there throughout the exercise. If you do these on an incline, bring your legs up and in close to your body and place your feet below your glutes on the bench.

Keep your elbows positioned close to the bench and near your body, and your arms turned out to your sides and away from your body. Keep them in this position throughout the exercise. You'll find this will help minimize cheating and will isolate the biceps more.

Seated Barbell or Dumbbell Preacher Curl

Keep your legs either locked behind you on the seat support or with only the tops of your toes touching the ground. Take your legs and feet out of the exercise so that your upper torso does the work.

Allow your upper body to lean forward and against the preacher bench arm pad as opposed to leaning back away from the pad. This way your upper body won't help cheat and make the exercise easier. You want only the biceps to do the work, not the legs, back, or delts.

ABS

Crunch

You can either position your legs so they are bent and resting on top of a flat bench or against a wall, or they can rest on top of a racked barbell if you do them while lying on a flat bench.

The important thing to remember as you come forward to crunch your upper torso is to allow your knees to come back toward your chest at the same time. You can really feel the difference doing crunches this way compared to doing them with bent legs in a nonmoving position.

You will be surprised to feel the difference it makes when someone holds your ankles in place.

Bicycle Crunch

This is quite similar to the regular crunch; however, as you come forward to crunch your upper torso, allow your knees to come back toward your chest at the same time and do small circular bicycle-pedaling motions when your upper body is up and closest to your knees.

For variation, you can do a straight forward crunch, a one-side-up/the-other-side-up alternating type of crunch, or a combination left-side/straight-forward/right-side bicycle crunch.

As with all ab work, especially crunches, use short-range movements of only a few inches from start to finish and keep the reps going without resting. This will make your abs burn and work them very effectively. Use high reps of 20 or more, and rest no longer than 15 to 20 seconds between sets.

Lying Knee Raise

I suggest doing these on a flat bench or platform that's at least one foot off the floor. Lie on your back with only your glutes and upper body on the bench. Place your hands, palms down, under your glutes. Keep both legs together and allow your legs to straighten out in front of you so that they are in a straight line with the upper body. Bend your knees and bring your legs up until your knees come to about stomach level. Contract your abs and slowly return your legs to the locked-out straightened position and repeat. Keep your legs completely off the floor from start to finish.

Seated Trunk Twist (Knees Up)

This is going to be strange at first, since it'll feel like you won't have much balance. But don't worry, you soon will.

Begin the bicycle crunch with knees bent and legs up.

Extend the right leg. As you bring it back, extend the left leg.

Many people prefer to do the lying knee raise on a bench as opposed to the floor.

Essentially, it is a seated trunk twist with a broomstick behind your neck but with your knees bent and feet off the floor.

Begin by doing them with your legs and feet completely extended and straight out in front so that only your heels touch the floor. Then work to make it a little harder by keeping your knees slightly bent and feet up off the ground. Finally, bend your knees more and bring your knees and legs up higher and toward your upper body.

You might be able to only do 1, 2, or 3 reps like this at first, but each time you do it, it'll get easier (at least you'll start to get the hang of it), until you'll be able to do side-to-side seated trunk twists with your knees up high and tucked close to your body. Talk about having great balance!

Training on the Ball

Are you ready for something completely different? This kind of training is probably so far removed from what you've always done that you'll think I'm off my rocker—but it works great.

Strong abs are essential to good balance as you will see with this exercise.

You're going to do some of your exercises on a big, inflatable ball. That's right, a ball. When you do regular training, your body is pretty much in a fixed position from start to finish, and you use a certain number and kind of muscles to help you do the lift. With the exception of a few variables (e.g., using heavier weights), those muscles probably didn't change very much, if at all. But with the ball, everything changes.

For example, one of the exercises you'll do on the ball is dumbbell flyes. On a flat or incline bench, those flyes were pretty easy and predictable. On a ball, just moving your legs forward or backward instantly changes your body position on that ball, and by doing so, you also change the degree and intensity of all the other muscles that come into play to help you complete that exercise. Perhaps in a certain position on the ball, you feel those flyes more in your lower chest. However, allow the ball to move back toward your calves and your upper body to slide down a bit, and you immediately change where the exercise hits you to the upper chest area. All that by just moving the ball and your body position a few inches at most!

I suggest using a good size ball that's about two to four feet in diameter so you can have plenty of room to place your upper body and to do the exercises. I suggest using one with ridges or a rough surface in order to maximize traction so it won't slip out from under you.

Obviously, you can't do every exercise for every bodypart on the ball, but here are some that work great.

CHEST

Chest Press Dumbbell or Barbell

Unless you've got a spotter to hand you a barbell, stick with dumbbells. They're a heck of a lot easier to pick up on each side once you get your upper body in place.

Be sure that your entire back is resting against the ball. Let the curve of your back conform to the curve of the ball. Do this exercise just like you do a regular chest press, but keep your elbows out and away from the ball as you press the weight up and down.

Your feet should be placed flat on the floor in front of you with your legs spread about one to two feet apart in order to create more stability. Begin doing the press in this starting position. After a few reps, let your legs slowly move the ball backward a few inches for a few reps, then forward a few inches for a few reps. Feel the difference? Remember which way you felt it more.

Once you get used to the ball, a little trick you'll want to use is changing how you place your feet. Instead of keeping them flat on the floor, keep your heels up and only your toes on the floor. This will allow you to move the ball effortlessly backward or forward a few inches in the middle of a set without having to stop and change foot and leg positions.

Dumbbell Flye

Do these just like you did the chest press, but instead of pressing the weights up, use a flye motion in a big semicircle type of arc. Keep your elbows back, and use lighter weights so you can get that big chest stretch.

BACK

Dumbbell Row

Who would've thought you could do rows on this thing? Well, you can, and it's pretty amazing how you'll feel these. This time, you'll face down with your stomach, instead of your back, on the ball. Let your upper body curve to the shape of the ball's curve.

Your feet should be one to two feet apart, and the balls of your feet should be on the floor. Keep your neck and head up and looking forward, and both should be up and off of the ball. Only your upper body up to your upper chest and lower neck should be touching the ball.

Holding two dumbbells in your hands and doing the exercise with both arms simultaneously will help keep you balanced throughout the exercise. Begin by bringing the weights up and your elbows above your upper torso and behind you. This will help you get a good back contraction. Lower the weights as far down as possible and repeat.

After a few reps like this, begin to move your feet so the ball moves backward a few inches and then forward a few inches. Do a few reps each way. Which way do you feel it more? Less? Once you get the hang of this, you'll be able to do a continuous set of stationary, backward, and forward reps without giving much thought to where and how you should move your body. Again, keep your toes flexible so that you can easily and quickly move the ball either backward or forward to find the "sweet" spot where you feel the exercise most. Remember, it'll only take a few inches to do that, too.

SHOULDERS

Bent-Over Dumbbell Lateral Raise

Place your legs, feet, and upper body in the same position as in the dumbbell row. Instead of rowing the weight up and back, you simply raise the weights up and out as far as you can to your sides. You can have a slight bend to your elbows, but not much. You want to make the delts work, and the farther the weights are out and away from your body, the harder they work and the more of a disadvantaged position (unable to help cheat) you put your arms in.

After a few reps like this, begin to move your feet so the ball moves backward a few inches and then forward a few inches. Do a few reps each way. Which way do you feel it more? Less?

Again, keep your toes flexible so that you can easily and quickly move the ball either backward or forward to find the "sweet" spot that you feel the exercise most. Remember, it'll only take a few inches to do that, too.

Do nonstop reps during each set, and don't allow the weights to come all the way down; keep a constant tension on the delts by keeping your arms and weights up at the bottom position. Feel the burn and you'll see the results.

Lying Dumbbell Lateral Raise

You'll do this in much the same way as you do the dumbbell bent-over lateral, but you'll place your body on its side and do one set at a time for each side. Your feet should be placed flat on the floor in front of you with your legs spread about one to two feet apart in order to create more stability. Your upper body will be slightly twisted because of the leg and foot position needed to create the greatest stability.

Begin doing the side laterals in this starting position.

After a few reps, let your legs slowly move the ball backward a few inches for a few reps, then forward a few inches for a few reps. Feel the difference? Remember which way you felt it more.

Once you get used to the ball, a little trick you'll want to use is changing how you place your feet. Instead of keeping them flat on the floor, keep your heels up and leave only your toes on the floor. This will allow you to effortlessly move the ball backward or forward a few inches in the middle of a set without having to stop and change foot and leg position.

Allow the ball to move forward and backward a few inches in order to let your upper body move up and down on the ball. Notice any difference in where you feel the exercise when your body is slightly lower on the ball as compared to when it's positioned up a little higher?

Also, keep the weight down, out in front of you, and away from the ball when you start the exercise. Bring the weight up and above your body in an arc until you feel a powerful contraction in your delts.

Remember these positions so you can go right to them for the next set. With any delt exercise, keep the delts working and burning. That means constant tension, nonstop reps, and very minimal rest between sets.

22

Workout 15: The Weak-Link Workout

Notice I didn't say *weakling* workout? That's because all of us have certain bodyparts or muscles that are weaker than others, and those weaker muscles are one of the big things that hold us back from reaching more success in our training. As they say, *you're only as strong as your weakest link*, and once you get on this workout, those weak links are going to be just a thing of the past.

You will use a type of training called dead-stops. Many of the world's best strength athletes have used this type of training for years and have watched their progress skyrocket as a result.

Weak-link, dead-stop training means training the weakest point in any given exercise. That is, at what point of the exercise do you find it the toughest? And don't you dare answer before you begin.

Let's take legs. Say you've had a tough go of getting your legs to grow or become stronger. What can you do? Two things: (1) use a power rack, adjust the rack pins, and do sets of quarter- and half-range movements; (2) without using the power rack, do a regular squat, but stop each rep at the bottom position for two seconds, then come back up and repeat.

These dead-stops will give you incredible power from the bottom position. You can also do power-rack and dead-stop training on presses and deadlifts with equally great results. *I suggest doing dead-stop and power-rack training once every two weeks.*

Let me give you a great weak-link, dead-stop workout for every bodypart.

LEGS

Squat

Do this just as I described above.

Stiff-Legged Deadlift (Barbell or Dumbbell)

Do quarter- to half-range movements from starting position to half lock-out. Then do another set of half- to full-lock-out reps. Do dead-stops at the bottom of the movement, too.

Leg Curl (Lying, Seated, or Standing)

Do quarter- to half-range movements from starting position to half lock-out. Then do another set of half- to full-lock-out reps.

Calf Raise (Seated, Standing, or Donkey)

Do quarter- to half-range movements from starting position to half lock-out. Then do another set of half- to full-lock-out reps.

CHEST

Flat or Incline Barbell Press (Smith Machine or Power Rack)

Set the pins in the power rack to allow only quarter- and half-range movements. On the Smith machine, do two-to-three-second dead-stops at the bottom of the exercise.

BACK (TRAPS)

Power-Rack Barbell Shrug

Set the rack pins high enough so that when you grab the barbell resting on top of the pins, you won't have to bend over to pick it up. That is, place the barbell high enough so that with your arms straight down and elbows locked out, you can grab the weight and shrug it up a few inches and then back down on top of the pins.

BACK

Deadlift in Power Rack

You'll set the pins lower than you did for the shrug—at about knee level. This will be the starting position for the

deadlift, instead of having to pick the weight up from the floor. Set the pins a few inches higher if you would like to do quarter-range reps. Setting the pins at knee level will allow you to do half-range reps and will really help strengthen those erectors, which will help your leg strength, especially for exercises like the squat, since your lower back (the support column that holds the weight) will now be much stronger.

SHOULDERS

Seated or Standing Barbell Press (Smith Machine or Power Rack)

The four to six inches before you lock your arms out is the strongest power range for the triceps, and doing quarter- and half-range movements will help build strength and power here. Yet, for many people who do full-range-rep training, the lowest point of the move-

Using quarter-, half-, three-quarter-, and full-range rep training will give you strength throughout all ranges of motion.

ment, where the weight is at the bottom and you need to power it up, is where they find they're the weakest and need the most help.

I suggest doing power starts from this position. You basically allow the weight to come all the way down and let it rest for a few seconds, then press it back up and repeat. This takes the momentum and cheat out of the exercise by essentially becoming two separate exercises: from the top to the bottom, then stop; from the bottom to the top, then stop.

BICEPS

Barbell Power-Rack Curl

I suggest setting the power-rack pins so that the barbell will be positioned at the halfway point of the regular full-range barbell curl. That is where your forearms will be roughly at lower chest and stomach area, about 90 degrees with the floor. This will be the starting point. From here, curl the weight up until the biceps are fully contracted. Don't allow the weight to come too far back toward your shoulders, since this will take the stress and work off the biceps. Slowly lower the weight and

repeat. For variety, do a few partial reps whereby you're only curling the weight up just a few inches before bringing it back down again.

TRICEPS

Flat Bench Barbell Press in Power Rack with Close Grip

Remember what you did in the power rack for the shoulder press? Well, you will do something quite similar, except this time you'll lie on a flat bench (just like doing a regular bench press) and the power-rack pins will be placed so that you can only press the barbell up about three to six inches above you.

These three to six inches before your arms are fully locked out are the strongest range for the triceps. Strengthening your triceps in this range of motion will help strengthen them for all ranges of motion, too.

I suggest experimenting with different hand spacing. Try shoulder-width to only six to eight inches apart. Feel which one hits you the best. Many people have found that the closer their grip, the more they feel it in the triceps. The wider the grip, the more they feel it in the chest.

23

Workout 16: The 17-Minute, Whole-Body Recharge Workout

Everywhere I go, people tell me they want to work out but they don't have much time. The one-set routine I gave you earlier in the book is one of many ways to work out with little time.

But what if you have almost zero time, yet you want and need a good whole-body workout. Are you out of luck? Not if you follow this 17-minute whole-body recharge workout.

In all the other workouts, you concentrated on working different bodyparts at a time. Sometimes you did straight sets for just one particular muscle group; other times you did several different compound sets (multiple exercises for the same bodypart) or you did supersets (one exercise for one bodypart followed by one exercise for its opposing muscle group, e.g., biceps and triceps).

This time, since time is the consideration, the emphasis will be on using big-muscle exercises, whenever possible, that will work many other muscles at the same time. For example, the bench press—incline, decline, or flat—will work the chest, shoulders, and triceps. Squats will work the quadriceps, lower back (keeping the

upper body erect), and shoulders (keeping the bar stabilized on top of your shoulders).

The key to making this very brief training work well for you is using higher training intensity. In this case, it means using heavier weights and a decreased rest time, since you also want to get your heart rate up to aerobic or near-aerobic levels and sustain it there during the entire workout. Many people don't realize how easily they can accomplish both types of training, aerobic and anaerobic, simply by *increasing* training intensity while *decreasing* rest time between reps, sets, and exercises, which ultimately decreases your total training time.

Here are the key points of this workout:

1. You'll begin with cardio training, but you will drastically reduce your cardio workout time while dramatically raising your cardio workout intensity.
2. You'll do one exercise that will work many muscle groups at the same time.
3. You'll rest no longer than 70 seconds before beginning your next exercise.
4. You'll use lower reps.
5. You'll use heavier weights.
6. You'll stretch after finishing the weight training part of the workout.

Each of the following workouts is designed to be finished in 17 minutes. You'll see the time allotted for each particular exercise in each workout and the muscle groups worked for the weight training part of the workout.

WHOLE-BODY RECHARGE WORKOUT 1: CARDIO

Treadmill, 5 Minutes Set the exercise program to manual, and after a one-minute warm-up (no incline and 3.5

Try this: Reduce your *time* on cardio by 50 percent and increase *intensity* by 50 percent.

mph), incline the treadmill to 10 to 15 degrees and raise the speed to 3.7 to 4.0 mph. Take big, brisk steps for three minutes at this elevated pace. Once the treadmill counter reaches the four-minute mark, decrease the incline to 3 degrees and the speed to 3.4 mph and continue walking until you reach the five-minute mark. At five minutes you're finished, and it's time to immediately move to weights.

WHOLE-BODY RECHARGE WORKOUT 1: WEIGHTS

Chest, Shoulders, Triceps

Barbell Bench Press (Flat or Decline), 2 Minutes Load a barbell that will allow you to do 6 to 9 reps at 85 percent of your maximum 6-rep weight. For example, if your best 6-rep bench press is 200 pounds, then put 170 pounds on the bar and do 6 to 9 reps with it.

Do 1 set. Rack the weight, unload the plates, and quickly move to the next exercise.

Back, Biceps

Reverse-Grip EZ-Bar or Barbell Row, 2 Minutes You'll find it easier to do this with the EZ-bar, so that would be my first choice. Either way, load an EZ-bar or barbell with the best weight you can do for 6 reps. Your knees should have a slight bend, and your upper torso should be bent over forward at roughly a 60- to 80-degree angle. Use a reverse grip (underhand), and you want to pull the weight up and into your waist and lower abs. Be sure to bring your elbows back behind you as far as possible so you will really contract your back muscles. Do 1 set. Rack or put down the weight, unload the plates, and quickly move to the next exercise.

Quads, Inner Thighs, Glutes, Hamstrings, Calves

Leg Press, 1 Minute You need to use a weight about twice as much as your bodyweight. On this exercise, you need to keep your feet wide on the platform and pointed outward. Always keep your knees in a straight line over your big toes while doing the reps. Stay tight in the seat, and don't allow your glutes to lift up and out of the seat when your legs and the platform come down. Come down as far as you can, and stop at the point you feel your glutes starting to rise up. Your feet and legs need to stay wide from start to finish in order to hit all the targeted muscles in the way you want to hit them. Do 1 set of 13 to 17 reps.

Leg Press Toe Raise, 1 Minute Immediately after the last rep, rack or secure the weight and change foot position. This time, you want to place the balls of your feet on the bottom edge of the

Leg press toe raises are a screamer calf exercise.

platform. Keep the weight pins or safety stops secured throughout this set. You'll do leg press toe raises for the calves, and this is a killer exercise if you do it right.

Keep your knees together and lock them out. You will only move your toes and ankles—nothing else. Slowly lower the platform until you really feel it stretch your calves. You should feel it in your calves and up higher behind your knees and lower hamstrings. Hold the platform in the lowered position for one to two seconds; then toe press the platform up until your calves are fully extended. Do 1 set of as many reps as possible. Rack the weight, unload the plates, and quickly move to the next exercise.

Abs

Crunch, 2 Minutes The good ol' crunch—still one of the best ab exercises around. Remember, the key to making the crunch a great ab toner is the constancy of tension on the abs from doing non-stop reps, and the short range of motion that helps increase the intensity of work.

I suggest keeping your feet and legs up and your knees bent back toward your upper body. Keep your head and neck continuously up and off the floor throughout the set. No letting those abs rest!

Do 1 set of 30 to 60 nonstop reps. You may even want to do one-third of your reps with more emphasis on your left side, one-third of the reps with emphasis on the right side, and the remaining one-third of the reps straight forward. After your last rep, quickly get up and finish your workout with the following good basic stretches.

Stretch

Lat Stretch, 30 Seconds Using one arm at a time, grab hold of a vertical bar on a machine. Lean back and hold it in the stretched position for 20 to 30 seconds. Feel it really stretch those lats. You'll also feel it stretch the biceps. Repeat for the other side.

Chest Stretch, 30 Seconds Using one arm at a time, grab hold of a vertical bar on a machine. This time, keep your upper body erect, and with your arm fully locked out, turn your upper body away from the opposite arm holding the vertical bar. You should really feel this in your pecs. Hold the stretched position for 20 to 30 seconds, then repeat for the other side.

Triceps Stretch, 30 Seconds On the same machine vertical bar, allow one side of your upper body to lean against it, letting that side's triceps lie flat against the bar. Try to place as much of your upper arm firmly against the vertical bar as you can. Bend your elbow so that your forearm and hand are bent over behind the arm. Lean into the vertical bar until you really feel your triceps stretch. Hold the stretched position for 20 to 30 seconds, then repeat for the other side.

This is one of the best chest stretches you can do.

If you have difficulty with this stretch, use your other hand to grab the wrist and pull down.

To increase the stretch in your quad, tip your pelvis forward slightly.

Quad Stretch, 30 Seconds Stand up with your body in a straight vertical line. Bend your knee until your calf and foot are behind you. With the same hand as the bent leg (e.g., left hand holding the left foot), grab the top of your foot and hold it until your heel touches your glutes. Keep the bent upper-leg in a straight line with your upper body. Hold it in the stretched position for 20 to 30 seconds, then repeat for the other side.

Hamstring Stretch, 30 Seconds Keep both legs together and feet pointed straight forward. Allow your upper body to bend forward until your chest comes down to upper-leg level and your head is at knee level. Grab hold of your ankles, and with a gentle but controlled pull, bring your upper body down as far as possible until you really feel a great stretch in your hamstrings. Don't bounce. Simply go as far as you comfortably can, and you'll find your range

of motion improving as you include this stretch in your routine on a regular basis.

Calf Stretch, 30 Seconds You already stretched your calves when you did the leg press exercise just described.

WHOLE-BODY RECHARGE WORKOUT 2: CARDIO

Stair Stepper, 5 Minutes You're going to like doing this exercise first, because you will not only take care of that cardio thing, but you will also give those calves of yours a great workout.

Here's what to remember. Keep your body straight up and down—leaning over or turning your hands and gripping outward on the rails. Only touch the rails if you need to regain your upper-body balance. Your hands and arms need to be free from holding on to the rails. As you step, move your arms just as you would if you were walking up and down a flight of stairs.

The next thing to remember is to keep only the balls of your feet on the back of the stepper. As each step goes down, let your heel come all the way down for a good stretch; then as the step comes up, let your heel come all the way up as high as possible to get a good calf contraction. These two things turn stair stepping into a fabulous calf exercise.

Now to get the most from the exercise for your glutes, hamstrings, and legs, be sure to take big, full steps all the way up and all the way down. None of this goofy few-inch-steps-done-very-quickly stuff you see so many people do. Big strides produce big results.

Set the exercise program to manual, just like on the treadmill. After a one-minute warm-up of moderate resistance, increase the resistance until you find just the right step cadence that allows you to come all the way up and down without going too fast or too slow. With so many different stair step machines out there, I cannot tell you where to find *your* cadence, but you can quickly find just the perfect spot you need. Do four minutes at this level until you've done a total of five minutes on the stair stepper. At the five-minute mark, stop, get off the machine, and hustle over to the weights.

WHOLE-BODY RECHARGE WORKOUT 2: WEIGHTS

Quads, Inner Thighs, Glutes, Hamstrings

Front or Smith Machine Squat, 2 Minutes
Your legs are already good and warmed up, so load the bar with just enough weight for you to do 1 set of 25 reps. Your feet should be a little wider than

Front squats force you to keep the torso upright.

shoulder-width and point outward and away from your body. Rest the bar on top of your traps and across the tops of your delts. Keep your upper body erect, and neck and head up and looking forward. Since your feet are so wide apart—think of how dancers point their legs outward—you won't need to go down to parallel position to get great results from these. Allow the bar to come down, all the while keeping your knees in a straight line over your big toes. Stop your descent just above the parallel position, and feel it really stretch your inner thighs and glutes. Power the bar up to the starting position, and repeat for 1 set of 25 reps. Rack the weight, unload the plates, and quickly move to the next exercise.

Lower Back, Hamstrings

Stiff-Legged Dumbbell Deadlift, 2 Minutes
You're going to take care of your lower back, traps, forearms, hamstrings,

and glutes with this one. Take a pair of dumbbells that are about 30 percent of your bodyweight (e.g., a 150-pound person would use 45-pound dumbbells).

Using as close to perfect form as possible is a must, not only to prevent injury, but to isolate the hamstrings and hit those deep muscle fibers. Here's how to do them.

Holding the weight with your arms locked out to your sides and your body fully erect, bend your upper torso over until the weights are lowered as far down as possible. Some people will be able to lower the weights to the tops of their feet. Others may only be able to bring the dumbbells down to shin level. You can bend your knees, but only slightly. You want to make sure the hamstrings are fully stretched. Do not round your back as you lower the weights. Keep your back flexed and tight, as this is not a lat movement. While keeping your arms locked out during the entire movement, bring your upper torso back up to the fully upright and erect position.

Always use a controlled movement throughout the whole rep. Never bounce or jerk your body or the weight. Keep the dumbbells close to your body from start to finish. Do 1 set of 6 to 9 reps. The big thing to remember is how you hold the dumbbells and where your arms and hands should be when you bend over. At the top of the movement, keep your upper body erect and the dumbbells to your sides. As you bend over, bring your arms around to the front of you until the dumbbells and your palms are facing your shins.

For a great hamstring stretch, on your last rep of your set, lower the dumbbells and keep them in the lowered position for 20 to 30 seconds. Keep both legs together and feet pointed straight forward. How far should you go down? Simply bring

your upper body down as far as possible until you really feel a great stretch in your hamstrings. Don't bounce. Go as far as you comfortably can, and you'll find your range of motion improving as you include this stretch in your routine on a regular basis.

Rack the weight and quickly move to the next exercise.

Chest, Shoulders, Triceps

Barbell or Dumbbell Incline Press, 2 Minutes

Pick a weight heavy enough for you to do 14 to 17 reps. And don't pick a light weight that makes it too easy to get those reps. For many people, the weight will roughly be about 35 to 40 percent of their bodyweight.

Keep your glutes tight against the seat and your back firmly against the backpad. Be sure to bring your elbows straight down toward the floor and not back behind you, and bring the dumbbells down until the dumbbell weight

To feel an even greater chest contraction, at the bottom of the movement (and not until then) bring your elbows slightly up and back.

plates are even with your chest. You must lower the weights down as far as possible in order to get a good stretch.

As you bring the weights back up and over you, don't allow the weights to touch each other. At the top of the movement, keep the weights about six to eight inches apart. After you've done 1 set of 14 to 17 reps, rack the weight and quickly move to the next exercise.

Back, Biceps

Reverse-Grip Straight-Bar Lat Machine Pulldown, 2 Minutes Use the same body position that you use for regular pulldowns with an overhand grip, except change your grip to underhand (palms facing your body instead of away) and let your hands be about 6 to 10 inches apart. Be sure to bring the weight down to lower chest level and your elbows straight back behind you so you can get a good back contraction. Allow the weight to come all the way up until your arms are fully extended above your head. Really go for the lat stretch. Do 1 set of 16 to 22 reps, then quickly move to the next exercise.

Abs

Hanging Knee Raises, 2 Minutes You will do these from a chin-up bar high enough off the ground so you can let your body fully hang straight without your feet touching the floor.

This is a great exercise for the lower abs. With your hands about shoulder-width apart, take an overhand grip on a chinning bar. Keeping your upper torso erect, raise your upper legs so that your knees come up and toward your stomach area. Really make the abdominals contract as your legs come up and your lower torso slightly bends forward and upward. Think of it like a U-shape. Lower and repeat. Do 1 set of as many reps as possible. Don't get dis-

couraged if you can't do very many at first. You will soon enough. After your set, quickly move to the last part of the workout.

Stretch

Lat Stretch, 30 Seconds It's called the chin-bar hang, and it works great for stretching those lats. Take an overhand grip on either a chin bar or Smith machine bar with the bar racked at the highest position on the machine. The preferable way is to use a bar high enough for your entire body to hang straight without your feet touching the floor. If this is not possible, then do these with your knees bent and your calves and feet behind you. The key is to let your arms fully extend and your upper torso hang so the lats will be stretched. Hang in this position for at least 20 seconds. If your grip will allow, hang a few seconds longer.

Chest Stretch, 30 Seconds This stretch will make use of the pec deck but only for support. Position yourself with your arms behind and resting against vertical pec-deck pads just like you would if you were doing the exercise. This time, instead of keeping your upper body firm against the backpad, let your upper body come forward while your arms remain immovable against the vertical pec-deck pads. Keep leaning forward until your arms are behind you and you really feel your chest stretch. Hold your body and your chest in this stretched position for 20 to 30 seconds.

Triceps Stretch, 30 Seconds Extend your right arm directly overhead. While keeping your upper arm close to your head, bend your elbow so that your forearm and hand are bent over behind your arm. With your left hand, grab your right hand that's behind your head and gently push down on it. You

Always stretch each bodypart before and after working it.

should really feel the triceps stretch when you do that. Hold the stretched position for 20 to 30 seconds, then repeat for the other side.

Quad Stretch, 30 Seconds Find a padded flat bench. Kneel down on top of the flat bench so that your legs are together and your glutes and upper-body weight rest on top of your calves, which are together behind and underneath you. Keep your upper body in a vertical, straight line, and slowly allow your upper torso to shift backward until you feel the stretch in your quad and upper thigh. Hold this position for 20 to 30 seconds. The more your upper body leans back toward your feet, the more you'll feel the stretch in your quads. To reduce the stretch, simply come up and forward.

Hamstring Stretch You already did the hamstring stretch at the end of the dumbbell stiff-legged deadlift workout.

Calf Stretch, 30 Seconds This is an easy one. Simply stand on the edge of a platform that's high enough for your heels to come all the way down as far as possible without touching the floor. Keep your body straight and only hold on to something for balance if you need to, but do not take your body-weight off the stretched calf muscles. This will really burn, and that's exactly what you want, so keep your powder dry. Hold the stretched position for 20 to 30 seconds.

WHOLE-BODY RECHARGE WORKOUT 3: CARDIO

Stationary Bike, 5 Minutes Adjust the seat high enough so that when the pedal is at the lowest or bottom position of the pedal stroke, your knee will only have a slight bend. Set the exercise program to manual, begin pedaling, and set the level of resistance to 2. Pedal at the rate

The purpose of a cardio machine is to elevate your heart rate and metabolism before your workout.

of 80 rpm for one minute at level 2. At the two-minute mark, change the level of resistance to between 6 and 10, depending on how easy or difficult it is for you. Always maintain at least 80 rpm. Exercise at levels between 6 and 10 until you reach the five-minute mark, then stop. You're finished and it's time to quickly move to the weights.

WHOLE-BODY RECHARGE WORKOUT 3: WEIGHTS

Quads, Inner Thighs, Glutes, Hamstrings

Machine Hack Squat, 70 Seconds Your legs should be already warmed up from the stationary bike, so it's time to make those legs burn even more. The machine hack squat is a great movement, especially when preceded by the bike.

Load enough weights on the machine to allow you to do 15 to 19 reps in good, strict form and heavy enough so that when you hit the fifteenth rep, your legs will be burning like crazy.

Vary the foot position, too. First of all, place your feet high up toward the top of the foot platform; you'll keep them in that general location, even when changing foot position.

If you do 15 reps, do 5 reps with your feet wide and pointed out and knees always traveling over the big toes; 5 reps with your feet about 8 to 10 inches apart and straight forward, but with your heels up and off the foot platform and all the weight centered over the balls and front of your feet; 5 reps with your knees and feet together and heels and toes on the platform.

You want to keep your legs moving on these by not stopping between reps or doing the reps too slowly. Picture your legs like a piston in an engine that is constantly moving up and down. Do 1 set and then quickly move to the next exercise.

Calves

Standing Toe Raise (with Bodyweight Only), 70 Seconds This is such a great calf exercise, and you don't even need a machine or any weight except your bodyweight. There are a few things to remember.

1. You need to get a great stretch at the bottom and a big contraction at the top of the exercise. Work the calf in its complete range of motion.
2. Put only the front balls of your feet on the standing platform so you can get this full range of motion.
3. Space your feet about 10 to 12 inches apart, and keep your knees close together and touching each other throughout the exercise.

The standing toe raise works great even with just your bodyweight.

4. Really focus on shifting your bodyweight so you can feel it over the big toes. This will help focus the calf work to hit the inner calf and will help you get that nice-looking diamond calf shape.

All that's left is doing the reps, so start repping up and down, up and down, until your calves really start burning. Don't stop until you've hit 40 to 60 reps. Go for more if you can. You'll find that as you do these bodyweight-only calf raises, not only will your calf shape change, but so will your ability to do more and more reps.

Do 1 set of 40 to 60 reps. Then, instead of waiting to stretch at the end of the workout, do your calf stretch immediately after your last rep—to really feel something intense. Stand on the edge of the same platform you used for the calf raise. Keep your body straight and only hold on to something for balance if you need to, but don't take your bodyweight off the stretched calf muscles. This will really burn, and that's exactly what you want. Hold the stretched position for 20 to 30 seconds. After the stretch, hobble, oops, I mean walk, as quickly as you can over to the next exercise.

Chest, Shoulders, Triceps

Dumbbell Flat Bench Press and Flye, 70 Seconds You'll do two slightly different chest exercises here. Pick a weight that you can do for 9 to 12 reps. Position your body on the flat bench so that your upper body is completely on the bench, and your legs and knees are bent, up and off the floor, and elevated above the flat bench. With palms facing forward, and arms and weights locked out above your head, slowly lower the weights down and out to your sides until your arms are in a straight line with your shoulders. This

will help you feel the exercise more in the chest. Your elbows should point down and a bit below the top of the flat bench. Then you know you're getting into big stretch territory. Go as far down as is comfortable. Press the weights back up to the top and repeat for a total of 8 reps.

After the eighth rep, turn your hands so that your palms now face each other and not forward like they did in the dumbbell press. It's now time for flyes. Bring your arms down like you did with the press, but this time, think of the movement like putting your arms around a big wide barrel. Get a nice, deep stretch at the bottom, and as you bring the weights up in a semi-circle, don't let them touch each other at the top of the exercise. Keep them about six to eight inches apart to keep a good contraction on the pecs. Do 8 reps. After the last rep, rack the weights and quickly move to the next exercise.

Back, Biceps

One-Arm Low-Pulley Cable Row, 70 Seconds You'll turn this into two different exercises simply by changing your hand position during the exercise. Take a stirrup-style handle attached to a low pulley. Load a weight heavy enough for you to do 11 to 14 reps. With your right side facing the weight stack, grab the handle with your left hand so that your palm is facing the floor, and allow your left arm to fully extend in front of you. With your knees bent and your upper body bent over, pull your arm back behind you. As you do, turn your hand so that your palm faces upward by the time your arm comes all the way back and your hand reaches your side. Remember, your palm faces down at the start and faces up at the end of the movement. Let your arm return to its starting position, and repeat for 11 to 14 reps. Switch arms and body position

Finally, a back exercise you can really feel that's fun to do.

To make this cable row effective, be sure to use proper form.

for the next side. After you've done 11 to 14 reps for each side, quickly move to the next exercise.

Lower Back, Hamstrings, Glutes

Hyperextension Bench, 70 Seconds This is such a great exercise and again, it only uses your bodyweight. On a hyper-bench, position your upper body so it doesn't touch the bench. You want it to move freely. With your arms in front of you and tucked near your chest, bend your upper torso until your head is near the floor. Hold this position for one to two seconds. Then slowly raise your upper torso until it is even and in a direct line with your legs. Do not hyperextend your upper body by allowing it to be raised higher than your legs. After doing 12 to 15 reps, immediately turn your body over, and you're ready for the next exercise.

Abs

Reverse-Body Hyperextension, 70 Seconds Your body position will be much like the hyperextension—only your lower body touching the bench—but this time you won't go down as far. Nowhere near as far, in fact, only a few inches.

Think of these like crunches, only this time your upper body will have to work against gravity since it won't have the floor to rest on. Besides, by now you've learned to keep your upper body elevated throughout the entire crunch. Allow your upper torso to come down only until it reaches the parallel straight-line position with your lower torso resting on the bench. Bend your head and chest upward and slightly forward, much like in a tucked position. Continue to bring your upper body up and forward in this tucked position

This is a terrific ab exercise, especially when you use a small range of motion.

until you feel a maximum contraction in the abs. This should only take a few inches of movement if you're doing it correctly. Hold this contracted position for two to three seconds; then slowly, and I mean slowly, lower your upper body back down a few inches, then right back up again. You should really feel your abs burn once you hit the 15-rep mark. Go for 1 set of at least 20 to 40 reps. After the last rep, move to the final part of the workout.

Stretch

Lat Stretch, 30 Seconds Remember the lat stretch in workout 2 that has your entire body hanging from a chin bar? Well, this one is somewhat like it, only you'll use a straight bar with stirrup handles at the ends or just a regular straight bar with a wide overhand grip.

Position yourself just like you would if you were doing regular lat pulldowns. This time, once you grab

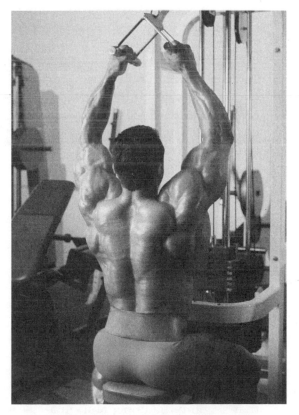

For an even better lat stretch, keep your arms locked and lean forward.

the bar and your arms are fully extended overhead, keep your arms there for 20 to 30 seconds. To feel the stretch even more, lean slightly forward and feel the difference.

To make this lat stretch work well, be sure to use a heavy weight. I suggest picking a weight that's equal to your bodyweight. Too light, you won't feel it; too heavy, you won't be able to pull the bar down far enough to sit down. Bodyweight seems to work well for this.

Chest Stretch, 30 Seconds You'll use the beginning phase of a cable crossover exercise for this stretch. Position your body in the middle of a pulley station. With your left hand grab the stirrup-style handle connected to the left upper pulley, and with your right hand grab the stirrup-style handle connected to the right upper pulley. Choose a weight that's roughly 25 percent of your bodyweight (e.g., if you weigh 200 pounds, use 50 pounds on both weight stacks). Allow your arms and the cables to fully extend up and out to your sides until your arms are completely extended and you feel a great chest stretch. To feel it even more, move your upper body slightly forward while your arms are fully extended. Hold this stretched position for 20 to 30 seconds.

Triceps Stretch, 30 Seconds If you can do the lying EZ-bar French press, then you'll easily be able to do this stretch. In fact, that's exactly the exercise you'll use, except instead of lowering the weight behind your head and extending it back up overhead, you'll simply lower the weight and keep it in the lowered position for 20 to 30 seconds. The big thing to remember is that keeping the upper arms in a locked position and the hands lowered as far down as possible really makes

the triceps stretch. Hold the weight in this lowered, fully stretched position for 20 to 30 seconds.

Quad Stretch, 30 Seconds Think of how you would do a regular barbell squat— body upright, head up and looking forward, upper bodyweight centered over the back of your heels, knees traveling in a straight line over your big toes, feet about shoulder-width apart—only you will not use any weight, just a good, deep knee bend. Lower your body until you reach the bottom position of the knee bend and squat. Keep it in the lowered position for 20 to 30 seconds.

Hamstring Stretch, 30 Seconds Time to use the barbell stiff-legged deadlift, which has almost the same form and body position as the dumbbell stiff-legged deadlift. Holding the weight with your arms locked out down against your legs and your body fully erect, bend your upper torso over until the barbell is lowered as far down as possible. Some people can lower the barbell until it touches the top of their feet. Others can only bring the barbell down to shin level. You can bend your knees, but only slightly. You want to make sure the hamstrings are fully stretched.

Do not round your back as you lower the weight. Keep your back flexed and tight, as this is not a lat movement. Keep the barbell in the lowered position for 20 to 30 seconds. Keep both legs together and feet pointed straight forward.

How far should you go down? Simply bring your upper body down as far as possible until you really feel a great stretch in your hamstrings. Don't bounce. Go as far as you comfortably can, and you'll find your range of motion improving as you include this stretch in your routine on a regular basis.

Calf Stretch, 30 Seconds Stand up straight. Place one or both hands against a wall. While keeping your upper body upright, bring your left leg back behind you about two to three feet; the entire surface of your left foot must be firmly flat on the floor. Now lean forward slightly until you feel a good stretch in the left calf. The farther forward your upper body goes, without moving your left foot, the more you'll feel the stretch in the left calf. Hold for 20 to 30 seconds, and repeat for the other side.

24

Workout 17: The Hot-Zone Workout for Women

The Four Bodyparts Women Want Most to Look Awesome:
1. Flat stomach
2. Tight, round glutes
3. Great-looking inner and outer thighs
4. Strong and shapely shoulders

Whether we like it or not, as men and women, society defines us by our bodyparts. Women seem to want certain bodyparts to look especially good while guys want others. Add the fact that society's favorite bodypart of the month changes so fast it makes your head spin. Just look at how quickly magazine covers and articles change each month. We have all those infomercial products that tell you abs are the magic muscle to make you look and feel good this month, only to hear in a few months the message to forget the abs, it's now legs. Who can keep up? Who wants to?

I'm a big believer in finding balance in our lives, and this is especially true when it comes to working out and building and toning our bodies. Still, women and men are going to want certain bodyparts to look better than others. And on many of the lists and polls that ask people what they would like to change about how they look, certain bodyparts are often found at the top for women and certain others for men.

To help you achieve the look *you* want, I've created two separate

workouts—one for women and one for men—that will focus specifically on these top-of-the-list bodyparts and will include some of the best exercises and workouts I've seen.

Let's start with the hot-zone workouts for women.

FLAT STOMACH AREA

Do one or two of the following ab exercises each workout, and make sure that each workout you do different exercises than you used for the previous workout. Don't rest between reps, and don't allow the abs to relax. The only rest the abs get should be the 15 to 20 seconds or so between sets and when you move to the next ab exercise. Think constant tension and short range of movement, and your abs will respond beautifully!

Rocking Crunch

- Lie on the floor or flat bench with your legs up, knees bent, and legs together.
- Raise your upper body and bring it forward toward your knees while at the same time bringing your legs up and back toward your chin.
- At the top position, your body should approach the shape of a U or V.
- On the next rep, don't bring your legs so far back, but bring your upper body farther forward as if you're trying to touch your knees with your upper body.
- On the third rep, don't bring your upper body so far up and forward; instead, bring your legs and knees back farther as if you're trying to touch your chin.
- The rep cadence goes first rep, equal distance up for lower and upper body; second rep, upper body farther forward and legs low-

ered but not touching floor; third rep, upper body lowered and not touching floor and legs and knees back trying to touch the chin.
- Do 4 sets of 30 reps—10 reps each way.

Bicycle Crunch

- This is quite similar to the regular crunch; however, as you come forward to crunch your upper torso, allow your knees to come back toward your chest at the same time, and do small, circular, bicycle-pedaling motions when your upper body is up and closest to your knees.
- For variation, you can do a straight forward crunch, a one-side-up/the-other-side-up alternating type of crunch, or a combination left-side/straight-forward/right-side bicycle crunch.
- As with all ab work, especially crunches, use short-range movements of only a few inches from start to finish and keep the reps going without resting. This will make the abs burn and work them very effectively.
- Do 4 sets of 30 to 50 reps, and rest no longer than 15 to 20 seconds between sets.

Lying Knee Raise

- Do these on a flat bench or platform that's at least one foot off the floor.
- Lie on your back with only your glutes and upper body on the bench.
- Place your hands, palms down, under your glutes.
- Keep both legs together and allow your legs to straighten out in front of you so that they are in a straight line with your upper body.

- Bend your knees and bring your legs up until your knees come to about stomach level.
- Contract the abs and slowly return your legs to your locked-out straightened position. Repeat.
- Keep your legs completely off the floor from start to finish.
- Do 4 sets of 20 to 30 reps.

Seated Trunk Twist (Knees Up)

- This will be strange at first, since it'll feel like you won't have much balance. But don't worry, you soon will.
- Essentially, this is a seated trunk twist with a broomstick behind your neck but with your knees bent and feet off the floor.
- Begin by doing them with your legs and feet completely extended straight out in front so that only your heels touch the floor.
- Then, work to make it a little harder by keeping your knees slightly bent and feet up off the ground.
- Finally, bend your knees more and bring your knees and legs up higher and toward your upper body.
- You might be able to only do 1, 2, or 3 reps like this at first, but each time you do it, it'll become easier (at least you'll start to get the hang of it) until you'll be able to do side-to-side seated trunk twists with your knees up high and tucked close to your body. Talk about having great balance!

Regular Seated Trunk Twist

Do these with a broomstick or no weight at all.

- Many people who use resistance (i.e., weights) find their waistline expanding instead of decreasing. This is simply because they're stimulating the muscles in the ab and waist area, which causes the muscles to get bigger and thicker instead of firmer, more toned, tighter, and smaller.
- You can do these either seated or standing.
- Place a broomstick behind your neck. With both hands gripping both ends, begin twisting from side to side.
- Start off by doing slow, limited-range-of-motion twists. Then, after one to two minutes of twisting, increase the tempo and range of motion. Do three to five minutes of continuous trunk twists.

TIGHT, ROUND GLUTES

You'll find many exercises and machines that will work the glutes, but the people I've helped have always found great results from doing a select few exercises. Here they are.

Squat

Earlier in the book you learned how to do this one, but there is a little trick that will shift the exercise emphasis to more glute and less leg if the glutes need a little help. The trick is to simply lean your upper body forward slightly as you do the reps. Keeping the upper body erect keeps the exercise emphasis on the upper legs, but bending slightly forward gives many people just enough exercise shift to feel the emphasis more in the glutes.

The other two factors that will help make the squat a great glute exercise are

1. Keep your feet firmly on the floor without elevating your heels. Elevated heels shift the exercise emphasis more to the quads, especially lower quads, depending on how high your heels are elevated.
2. The depth of your reps also affects how much of the glutes will be

worked. Experiment and determine where you feel the emphasis most. Many people find that the lower they go—even slightly below parallel—the more they feel the exercise hit the glutes.

Try a combination of low and high reps from 6 to 25 and do 2 to 4 sets.

Wide-Stance Deadlift

You will perform this just like a regular deadlift, only your hand and leg position will be different.

- Place your feet wider than shoulder-width with your toes pointed slightly outward and toward the inside of the weight plates.
- Take either a combination overhand and underhand grip or both-hands-over grip, about six to eight inches apart on the middle of the bar.
- Keep your legs bent, bar close to your shins, upper body erect, and head up and looking forward.
- Keep your arms locked out, and drive the weight up with your legs.

- If necessary, your upper body will lock out into the straight, vertical position at the end phase of the movement. Make your legs do the majority of the work.
- Do 3 to 4 sets of 5 to 7 reps.

Dumbbell Deadlift Between Legs

You'll use a very similar style to the wide-stance deadlift, only you'll use one dumbbell instead of a barbell.

- Use the same body position as the wide-stance deadlift.
- With both hands, hold a dumbbell between your legs.
- Be sure to keep your arms locked and both hands wrapped around the middle of the dumbbell's knurling.
- Again, keep your upper torso erect and let your legs do the work.
- Do 3 to 4 sets of 12 to 16 non-stop reps.

With upper body erect, lift only with the legs. Exhale on the way up and inhale on the way down.

Begin with knees bent, upper body erect, and head up. Grip the bar between your legs and take a deep breath.

Dumbbell Walking Lunge

Remember these steps: one leg steps forward, the other leg kneels down; then the other comes up and steps forward and the opposite leg kneels down. Here are a few other things to do.

- Hold a dumbbell in each hand, and keep the weights always close to your body.
- Keep your upper body erect from start to finish.
- Use straight-line steps, and be sure to bring your knee directly over the foot that steps forward.
- On the leg that kneels down, keep the upper leg in a straight line under the upper torso.
- Don't allow the kneeling leg's knee to touch the floor.
- Take big steps forward. The bigger the step, the more you'll feel the exercise working the glutes.
- Do 3 to 4 sets of 15 to 20 steps for each leg.

Barbell or Smith Machine Stationary Lunge

Think of doing this with much the same leg position as in the dumbbell walking lunge, except you'll use a barbell or Smith machine. And instead of walking forward, you'll basically stay in one position and only move one leg back and forth at a time.

- Keep your upper body and kneeling leg in an upright position.
- Lunge forward only as far as you can go while keeping your upper body and kneeling leg in this straight-up-and-down position.
- Do all your reps for one leg before changing legs and doing the other side—none of this one leg forward, then the next leg forward stuff.
- Do 3 to 4 sets of 13 to 19 nonstop reps.

INNER THIGHS

Wide-Stance Barbell or Smith Machine Ballet-Type Squat

The Smith machine is much easier to use for this exercise because much of the movement depends on balance.

- Stand like you would when doing a regular squat.
- Keep the bar up high on traps and lower neck.
- Space your legs wide and turn your feet out as far as possible.
- Try to keep your legs and feet as directly under the bar as you can.
- Be sure your knees travel in a straight line over your big toes from start to finish.
- Bend your knees and descend until your legs are about 3 to 4 inches above parallel.
- Return to the starting position and do 3 to 4 sets of 11 to 16 reps.

Leg Press (Feet Wide)

- The wider the foot position, the more you'll feel the exercise work the inner thighs.
- Do these much the same way you do your favorite leg press, except keep your feet wide and toes pointed outward and placed high on the foot platform.
- You'll also find that the deeper you allow the platform and weights to come down, the more you'll feel it work the inner thighs.
- Also, go for nonstop reps to keep the inner thighs burning.
- Do 3 to 4 sets of 15 to 25 reps.

Barbell or Machine Hack Squat (Feet Wide)

Continuing with the theme of feet placed wide, you can either use a barbell or hack squat machine for this.

- For barbell, elevate your heels on a one- to two-inch block or weight plates.
- Let your feet stand at about shoulder-width, and turn your toes slightly outward.
- Hold the barbell directly under and against the glutes and upper leg throughout the entire exercise. Do not let the bar move from touching the glutes—keep it there the whole time.
- Keep your arms locked and upper body erect, and descend until your legs are a few inches above parallel.
- Do 3 to 4 sets of 10 to 13 reps.

Seated Double Cable Squeeze (Arms Inside of Thighs)

You need to sit on a stool or the end of a flat bench for this one.

- Place the stool or flat bench in the middle of two low-pulley stacks.
- While sitting on the end of the bench or stool, grab with each hand a stirrup-style cable handle attached to the low pulleys.
- Spread your legs, but keep your heels together and off the floor. Only the balls of your feet will touch the floor.
- While holding the handles, lock your arms out and bring them inside your legs so they rest against the inside of your thighs.
- Keeping your upper torso erect and using only your legs—not your arms—squeeze your legs together until your arms touch each other.
- Slowly allow your legs to spread out again.
- Do 3 to 4 sets of 13 to 18 non-stop reps.

Forget infomercial gadgets or other machines—this cable exercise for the inner thighs is amazing and so are the results.

The only thing you want to move is your thighs.

OUTER THIGHS

Squats (Legs Together)

Here's a little trick to remember whenever you work your legs. By simply changing foot position, you change where the exercise will hit the muscle. Feet wide hits inner thighs; feet together hits outer thighs. So where do you think squats with feet together will hit? That's right, outer thighs. Here's a few other tips to help.

- One set, elevate your heels on a block or a pair of 25-pound plates. Next set, use no heel elevation. Which way do you feel it most? Where did you feel the differences?
- Use nonstop near-lock-out reps. The trick is to keep your legs constantly burning. You do this by stopping each rep about three-quarters of the way at the top, then going back down again for the next rep.
- Do 3 to 4 sets of 15 to 25 nonstop three-quarter reps.

Leg Press (Feet Together)

Here we go again with feet together to hit those outer thighs.

- Do one set with your feet high on the platform, one set with your feet positioned in the middle of the platform, and one set with your feet low on the platform. How did you feel each set? Where did you feel it?
- Change seat position, too. One set, have the seat all the way declined. Another set, raise the seat a few notches. Keep your feet in the same position when moving the seat. You want to find out if there are any differences in the way you feel the

exercise when you adjust your body position by moving the seat. Once you've determined that, then change your foot position on the platform, and use the combinations where you feel the exercise best.

- Do 3 to 4 sets of 18 to 22 nonstop three-quarter reps.

Hack Squats (Knees Together)

Use the same foot position suggestions as for the leg press. But also use these tips.

- One set, keep your upper body against the hack squat backpad. Next set, lift your glutes and lower back off of the backpad so that your legs come farther forward over the knees. Which way do you feel it best?
- Do 3 to 4 sets of 16 to 20 nonstop three-quarter reps.

Standing Side Leg Raise (Knee Bent and Bodyweight Only)

Forget about having to secure a strap attached to a low pulley around your ankles. Simply use your bodyweight—it'll work great.

- Stand erect and with your right hand hold a vertical bar on a machine for balance.
- Raise your left leg up and directly out to your left side.
- Bend your leg so that your calf and foot face behind your body.
- While keeping your upper body erect, raise your left leg up as far as possible. Go for waist level, if you can. If you're really limber, try to go a bit higher, but keep your upper body upright throughout the exercise.
- Keep your leg bent and behind you as you lower and raise your

The key is to keep the upper body erect and move only the leg you're working.

This side, leg, and hip exercise uses only your bodyweight and you can do it anywhere, anytime.

knee, and don't let it touch the floor until you've done 20 reps.

■ Do 3 to 4 sets of 20 nonstop reps per side.

STRONG AND SHAPELY SHOULDERS

Standing or Seated Dumbbell Lateral Raise (Side, Front, and Bent-Over)

Relax. You don't need to lift heavy weights to get shapely and strong shoulders. And put away those shoulder pads that you've tucked inside your tops. You'll soon not need them. The shoulders respond especially well to nonstop reps and reps without full lock-outs, though on one of the following exercises I'll have you do a full lock-out.

■ Since the shoulders (deltoids) comprise three separate muscles (front, side, and rear), by simply changing your upper-body position, you can work all three with the same exercise.

■ Begin with front raises and do one arm at a time. Keep your upper body erect, and with your arm fully extended, raise the dumbbell up and directly out in front of you until it comes to shoulder level. Hold it there for one to two seconds, then slowly lower it and do the same for the other side. Do 8 to 10 reps.

■ After the last rep, bring the dumbbells down to your sides, and then raise both arms up and directly out to your sides so that the weights and your arms are in a straight line with your upper body. You can have a slight bend at the elbows, but not much. Do 8 to 10 reps.

■ After the last rep, lower the weights down and bend your upper body forward. If you're seated, your upper body will be over your legs. If you're standing, your upper body will be bent over at about 80 to 90 degrees.

■ Bring your arms and the weights up and out to your sides, just like you did in the last exercise of side laterals. Do 8 to 10 reps.

■ Do 2 to 3 compound sets of these three nonstop delt exercises.

Standing or Seated One- or Two-Arm Dumbbell Press

For the one-arm version, do this exercise with your free arm holding on to the top of an incline bench or vertical bar for support.

■ Keep your body erect.
■ Holding the dumbbell in one hand, keep your palms facing forward and let the weight rest at shoulder level.
■ Press the weight up directly overhead until your arm is locked out.
■ Lower the weight to the starting position and repeat.
■ Do 3 to 4 sets of 11 to 14 reps.
■ Be sure that you come all the way down and your arms are fully

Most women prefer dumbbells to barbells for this exercise. Either one will give you great results.

extended at the top with the weight over your head.

Bent-Over Weight Plate Raises

These are much like the bent-over dumbbell laterals I told you about earlier; however, instead of using dumbbells, you will hold on to and use just the barbell plates.

■ If you can, use the kind of weight plates that have grip holes. If not, simply choose a weight that you can pinch and hold with your fingers throughout the entire set.
■ Your body position will be like it is for the bent-over dumbbell laterals; however, your arm position will change.
■ Begin the first few reps of the set with your arms out to your sides like in the bent-over dumbbell laterals. After a few reps, move your arms slightly forward and in front of you, and do a few reps. After a few reps like that, bring your arms out in front of you and do another few reps.
■ With each rep, keep changing your arm position and pay attention to where you feel the exercise hit your shoulders the best.
■ Do 3 to 4 sets of 16 to 23 continuous nonstop reps.

Regular and Reverse Cable Lateral

This is a lot like the dumbbell side and bent-over laterals except you'll use cables instead of freeweights.

■ For regular side or bent-over laterals, stand with your left side facing the cable machine, and with your right hand hold the low-pulley cable with a stirrup-style handle. The cable will be in front of your body.

- Keeping your body erect, raise your right arm until it comes up to shoulder-level. Lower your arm all the way down and repeat.
- After you've finished all the reps for that arm, turn your body around (right side facing the cable machine and left arm holding the cable handle), and complete the same number of reps on that side.
- Do 3 to 4 sets of 13 to 17 continuous nonstop reps for each side.
- Reverse cable laterals will work the rear deltoids. You'll use both cables at once.
- Position your body in the middle of two high-pulley cable machines.
- With your left hand grab the right cable, and with your right hand grab the left cable. Your arms should be crossed in front while holding both cables.
- Bend your upper body slightly forward (65 to 80 degrees), and extend your arms straight out away from your body.
- I prefer doing these with the arms bent and keeping that locked, bent position from start to finish. I think you'll find this will help you focus the work on the deltoids without having to constantly think about where your arms should be.
- Do short-range reps; perhaps only a few inches is all you'll need to really feel this exercise work those shoulders.
- Do a few reps with your upper body bent over in the lower starting position. Then after a few reps, raise your upper body a bit and do a few reps at that angle. Experiment and find at which upper-body angle your shoulders feel the exercise most.
- Do 3 to 4 sets of 13 to 17 continuous nonstop reps for each side.

25

Workout 18: The Hot-Zone Workout for Men

The Four Bodyparts Men Want Most to Look Awesome:
1. Chest
2. Arms
3. Shoulders and back (V-taper)
4. Abs

I know a lot of guys out there who think they're immune to all the craziness about body image that women go through. But I'm here to tell you, these guys are just as influenced by what society, women, and other guys think about them. And much of that is concentrated on how they look. Guys have favorite bodyparts, just like women, that they want to build and look good. That's fine, as long as there's a sense of balance not only to the look, but also to the approach to getting it.

I've seen guys with incredible upper bodies but legs so thin and small that they looked like pigeons. I've also seen guys with huge thighs but a narrow upper body that resembled a bowling pin.

I cowrote a book with the legendary movie star of *Hercules* fame, Steve Reeves. I don't know if you've ever seen pictures of this guy, but in his heyday, he had a physique—a *natural* one—like no other. Reeves's philosophy was balance: the arms, calves, and neck at all the same measurement. And boy did he ever have that "classic physique"

V-taper—the one you can get by using the exercises I'm about to give you.

Over the years, guys have told me the great-looking bodyparts they want most are chest, arms, shoulders, and back for that narrow waist, V-tapered look, and of course, great-looking abs.

Ab exercises are great and will definitely help anyone's physique, but bringing the abs out where they're very visible is done through reducing one's bodyfat percentage. That means doing more and eating slightly fewer calories than your body needs on a daily basis. This slight calorie deficit (with the right nutrients in the right combinations) will help the body burn excess fat. And since the ab exercises I gave the women for their hot-zone workout are so good, they'll work just as impressively for the guys.

I've seen so many guys respond so well to the three and four exercises I will give you for each bodypart, that I think you'll be one of them too. Choose any two exercises for each bodypart. On most of the exercises, you'll train heavy with lower reps, so two exercises will be more than enough to get those muscles working hard and getting stronger and bigger. Always do two different exercises for the same bodypart each workout. Mix up the combinations you use. Always doing something a little different will help keep you motivated.

Let's start off with the chest.

CHEST

Dumbbell Incline Press

You will focus your chest work on inclines because in my book, the incline press is superior to the flat bench press. I've seen many guys who have done the flat bench press for years, and while they have impressive mid-to-lower chest development, their upper chests always lagged behind. Yet I've also seen guys who've done mostly incline work, and their entire chests—from top to bottom—are big, thick, and complete. So if you're putting a lot of work into getting that chest looking great, why not make your time count and do the one type of exercise—inclines—that will produce complete results in one movement.

Use the following dumbbell incline tips for the barbell incline press as well.

- Use a fixed incline bench that's roughly 25 to 40 degrees, or set the incline bench at such an angle.
- The higher the incline, the more the work shifts to the shoulders. Keep the incline high enough so it's not a flat bench, yet low enough to keep the work centered more on the chest and not the delts.
- Keep your glutes firmly in the seat, and your upper body and head against the incline bench. Your feet should be flat on the floor and spread fairly wide for more stability and support.

- Bring the dumbbells up over your face until your arms are fully extended.
- Slowly lower the weights until they are at chest level.
- Be sure to keep your elbows at or near shoulder level and pointed back behind you. Keeping the elbows at this level seems to make the chest work harder and gives it a good stretch.
- Bring your arms and the weights up again until your arms are fully extended, but don't let the dumbbells touch each other at the top. Keep them about six to nine inches apart.
- Do 3 sets of 6 to 9 reps.

Barbell Incline Press

Use the same tips as for the dumbbell press, with these exceptions.

- Use a slightly wider than shoulder-width hand spacing on the barbell.
- Be sure to fully extend the barbell directly over your face until your arms are fully extended. Really squeeze and contract your chest when your arms reach this position.
- Lower the barbell until it actually touches the top of your chest and lower neck. Make sure your elbows are up high and pointed back as far as possible in order to get a great stretch.
- Do 3 sets of 6 to 9 reps.

Wide-Arm Push-Up (Feet Elevated Above Body)

You'll use only your bodyweight, but done correctly, this can be a great chest exercise.

- Place your feet so the top of your toes or shoes rest on a flat surface that's elevated about one to two feet off the ground.

- Only your feet and not any other part of your legs should touch the flat bench.
- Place your arms and hands at shoulder level, spread about a foot wider than shoulder-width.
- Keep your palms flat on the floor and fingers facing forward.
- While keeping your upper body in a straight line with your legs, bend your elbows so that your body lowers until it's about one to two inches away from touching the floor.
- Hold your body in the lowered position for one to two seconds, then bring your body up by extending your arms until they are locked out.
- Squeeze and contract your chest at the top. Hold this contraction for one to two seconds, then repeat.
- Do 3 sets of at least 10 reps and more, up to 20 if possible.

ARMS—TRICEPS

Seated Dumbbell French Press

This is like doing squats for the arms. This will do more for your triceps than the majority of other triceps exercises out there. Be sure to warm up thoroughly before jumping to the heavier weights.

I suggest doing about 2 to 3 light-to-moderate-to-moderately-heavy sets of 10 to 15 reps before handling the big poundages. If you need an extra warm-up set or two, go ahead and do them. You must warm up the triceps, elbow, and connective tissue areas before going any further.

- After the warm-up, add about 20 to 30 pounds to your highest warm-up weight and make that your first regular set.
- Use either a small pressing seated bench or use the 90-degree steep

side of a preacher bench. Be sure that the backpad covers most of your back for support and stability.
- Take a dumbbell, flip it on its end, and grab with both hands the inside of the upper plates. Your hands should be holding the underneath of the plates and your thumbs should be wrapped securely around the dumbbell bar.
- Raise the weight above your head with your arms fully extended.
- While keeping your upper arms close to your head, bend your elbows and lower the weight behind your head until it goes down as low as possible. Go for the fullest stretch you can.
- While still keeping your upper arms close to your head, extend your arms and weight back up overhead and lock your arms out. Really squeeze and contract the triceps and make them work.
- Repeat and do 3 sets of 6 to 9 reps.

Lying EZ-Bar French Press

Another great triceps movement, but the position of your arms is crucial to making it really work.

- Take an EZ-bar and lie down with your back on a flat bench.
- Place your head at the very end of the bench, but keep your head and neck on the bench.
- Raise the weight overhead, and bring your upper arms down and close to your head.
- Bend your elbows and lower the weight down and behind your head. Don't do what people call nose crunchers, where they lower the weight right above the face. The way I want you to do them is much more effective.
- As you bring the weight down, allow your upper arms to move

down toward the floor behind you and below your head.

- Keep your upper arms there as you extend your hands up and lock your elbows.
- The finish position will look like your arms are locked out behind your head at an angle of about 30 to 45 degrees.
- Keep your upper arms in this 30- to 45-degree-angled position for the rest of your reps.
- Do 3 sets of 12 to 16 nonstop reps.

Close-Grip Bench Press

You'll do this just like a regular bench press, except your hand spacing and elbow positions will be different.

- Place your hands toward the center of the barbell about 6 to 10 inches apart.
- Bring the barbell down to midchest level, and let the bar actually

If you're looking to put some major size and power into those arms, look no further than the close-grip bench press.

touch your body at the bottom of the exercise.

- Keep your elbows tight and close to your lats as you do each rep. This will help give you more power and stability, and it's the way many great powerlifters do their heavy bench presses.
- Be sure to lock your arms completely out once the weight is overhead. Feel the big triceps contraction.
- Do 3 sets of 5 to 9 full-range reps, and do a few short-range reps (only a few inches down, then up) once you can no longer do any more full-range reps.

ARMS—BICEPS

Seated Dumbbell Incline Curl

Where the arms are placed will most definitely affect where and how much you'll feel this exercise.

- Use a 40- to 45-degree bench.
- Sit firmly in the seat with your glutes and back always against the seat and backpad throughout the exercise.
- Holding two dumbbells, allow your arms to fully extend below you.
- Keep your upper arms against the sides of the incline bench.
- Begin with your palms facing each other in the lower position.
- Bend your elbows and raise the weights up and out away from your body, as if they're being raised out to your sides and away from you.
- Bring the dumbbells up high but only to the point where you feel the maximal contraction in the biceps.
- Hold the weights at this point for one to two seconds, then slowly lower the weight until your arms

Dumbbell incline curls force the biceps to work in ways that produce major results.

The EZ-bar takes the strain off your wrists and allows you to lift more weight than with a straight bar.

are fully extended below you. Always go for the full stretch at the bottom and full contraction at the top.

- Do 3 sets of 5 to 9 reps.

Standing EZ-Bar Curl

You'll find that you can curl a heck of a lot more weight with an EZ-bar than a regular barbell. The EZ-bar not only takes the stress off the wrists since your hands are at a more comfortable position, but it feels a bit different because your hands are closer together and closer to the center of your body.

- Keep your upper body erect, and if you must, only bend your knees very slightly, otherwise keep those legs straight.
- Keep your elbows and upper arms tucked close to your sides from start to finish.
- Take a fairly close grip on the EZ-bar and your palms will be facing

upward, albeit, slightly turned toward each other.

- Curl the weight up until you feel your biceps fully contract. Going back any farther toward the front delts will take the stress off the biceps.
- Lower the weight until your arms are fully locked out and the weight touches your thighs.
- Do 3 sets of 5 to 7 reps.

Thumbs-Up Cable Curl with Rope

For hitting the brachialis, that little muscle that sits under the biceps, this one is tough to beat. Most guys want the big biceps but don't do much to work the brachialis. (Think of it as the foundation upon which the house, the biceps, sits.) But working the brachialis will make those arms grow.

- You can use a V-bar if you can't find a rope, but the rope works better.

Thumbs-up rope curls really make the biceps work.

It's tough to beat the dumbbell press for shoulders.

- Stand about 12 to 18 inches away from a low-pulley machine.
- Grab hold of each end of the rope that's connected to the low pulley.
- While keeping your elbows and upper arms close to your sides and keeping your thumbs up, curl the rope up until you reach full contraction of the biceps.
- Keep your thumbs in the up position from start to finish.
- Always lower the weight until your arms are locked out and fully extended below you.
- Nonstop reps work great on this, so do 3 sets of 12 to 20 nonstop reps.

SHOULDERS, BACK (V-TAPER)

Seated Dumbbell Press

To put big, thick, wide delts on a guy's physique, there's just no getting away from heavy presses. One of the most effective exercises I've found for this is the seated dumbbell press. Dumbbells, more so than barbells, allow for freer movement and also a slightly greater range of motion, which can make all the difference between feeling the exercise a little or a lot.

- Use an incline bench that you can fully elevate so the backpad is nearly straight up and down at almost 90 degrees.
- I like just a very slight incline from vertical (perhaps one notch back) because it gives just a bit more freedom to find the most comfortable exercise groove to do the presses.
- With your body snugly against the seat and backpad and a dumbbell in each hand, bring the dumbbells up until they reach shoulder level. As soon as they reach that level, go ahead and press them up and directly over your head.

- Don't clang the dumbbells together at the top. Keep them about four to six inches apart.
- Lower the weights, and as you do, keep your arms in a straight line with your upper body and the elbows pointing straight down. Bring the weights down until they reach shoulder level, then press them up again.
- Some people will find great results by locking the elbows out at the top. Others feel the exercise more by pressing the weights up to near lock-out. Find out which of the two works better for you.
- Do 3 sets of 6 to 9 reps.

Chin-Up

Over the years, chin-ups have helped many, many guys to widen out. As an eight-time Mr. Olympia once told me, "It's one thing to do a lat pulldown, but there's nothing like pulling your whole body up and down in a chin-up." Absolutely.

Chin-ups can be tough, but they produce great results. Just hang in there if you're not able to do a bunch of reps right away. They'll come. And if you ever wonder if chin-ups are really that effective, just remember that the Navy SEALS, Special Operations Forces, and the rest of the military units train and test their soldiers on chin-ups, not lat pulldowns.

- Take a wider than shoulder-width overhand grip on a chin bar.
- Bend your knees and raise your calves and feet so they are behind your body.
- Pull yourself up until your chin is at or near the chin bar. Go higher to upper-chest level, if you can.
- As you reach the top, concentrate on keeping your elbows back behind you. This will help give you a better lat contraction.

- Slowly lower your body until your arms are fully extended and you feel a great lat stretch.
- Repeat and do 3 sets of as many reps as you can do.
- Once you can no longer do full-range reps, do a few short-range reps each set.
- If you can only do 2 to 3 full-range reps and the rest partial or short-range reps, then do them. You want to make your body stronger and used to the movement, and the only way to do that is by simply doing it. It may not look pretty, but very quickly, you'll become stronger.

T-Bar Row

T-bar rows did more for building and widening my back than any other exercise. You might find that they'll do the same for you.

- Load a T-bar row with enough weight for you to do at least 5 but no more than 8 reps.
- Place your feet close to the T-handle. Once you grab the handle, your hands will be only a few inches higher and forward of the tops of your feet.
- Bend your knees until your upper body is bent forward over the weight plates and it reaches the near-flat parallel position to the floor.
- Take an overhand grip on each side of the T-bar that's about six to eight inches apart.
- With your legs and upper body locked in position, bring the weight up to your chest by bringing your arms and elbows back behind you.
- Let the weight touch your chest, then lower it all the way down until your arms are fully straight and locked out. Really feel the lats stretch.

- Do not round your back at the bottom. Even when your arms and the weight are at the lowest point of the rep, keep your back flat and parallel to the floor.
- Do 3 sets of 5 to 8 reps.

Wide-Grip Barbell Upright Row

I'll show you how to turn this trap exercise into a great side deltoid movement all at the same time.

- Take a very wide overhand grip on a barbell. Your hands should almost touch the inside of the closest weight plates.
- Keep your body erect.
- Lower the barbell all the way down in front of you.
- Instead of allowing it to rest against your body at the bottom starting position, move the barbell away and in front of your body about four to six inches.
- Once you do that, you'll immediately feel the delts working.
- Keeping the bar always about four to six inches away from your body, raise your arms up and elbows high and raise the

barbell until it reaches chin or nose level.
- Hold it there for one to two seconds, then slowly lower it. Do not let the bar come any closer than four to six inches from your body during the entire exercise.
- Do 3 sets of 12 to 16 reps.

ABS

Do one or two of the following ab exercises each workout. Make sure you do two different ones than you used for the previous workout. Don't rest between reps, and don't allow the abs to relax. The only rest the abs should get is the 15 to 20 seconds between sets and when you move to the next ab exercise. Think constant tension and short range of movement, and your abs will respond beautifully!

Rocking Crunch

- Lie on the floor or flat bench with your legs up, knees bent, and legs together.
- Raise your upper body and bring it forward toward your knees, while at the same time bringing your legs up and back toward your chin.
- At the top position, your body should approach the shape of a U or V.
- On the next rep, don't bring your legs so far back, but bring your upper body farther forward as if you're trying to touch your knees with your upper body.
- On the third rep, don't bring your upper body so far up and forward. Instead, bring your legs and knees back farther as if you're trying to touch your chin.
- The rep cadence goes first rep, equal distance up for lower and upper body; second rep, upper

Moving your grip from close to wide turns a great trap exercise into a fabulous side delt movement.

body farther forward and legs lowered but not touching the floor; third rep, upper body lowered and not touching the floor, and legs and knees back toward the chin.

- Do 4 sets of 30 reps—10 reps each way.

Bicycle Crunch

- This is quite similar to the regular crunch; however, as you come forward to crunch your upper torso, allow your knees to come back toward your chest at the same time. Do small circular bicycle-pedaling motions when your upper body is up and closest to your knees.
- For variation, you can do a straight forward crunch, a one-side-up/the-other-side-up alternating type of crunch, or a combination of left-side/straight-forward/right-side bicycle crunch.
- As with all ab work, especially crunches, use short-range movements of only a few inches from start to finish and keep the reps going without resting. This will make the abs burn and work them very effectively.
- Do 4 sets of 30 to 50 reps, and rest no longer than 15 to 20 seconds between sets.

Lying Knee Raise

- Do these on a flat bench or platform that's at least one foot off the floor.
- Lie on your back with only your glutes and upper body on the bench.
- Place your hands, palms down, under your glutes.
- Keep both legs together and allow your legs to straighten out in front

of you so that they are in a straight line with your upper body.
- Bend your knees and bring your legs up until your knees come to about stomach level.
- Contract the abs and slowly return your legs to the locked-out straightened position and repeat.
- Keep your legs completely off the floor from start to finish.
- Do 4 sets of 20 to 30 reps

Seated Trunk Twist (Knees Up)

- This will be strange at first, because it'll feel like you won't have much balance. But don't worry, you soon will.
- Essentially, it is a seated trunk twist with a broomstick behind your neck but with your knees bent and feet off the floor.
- Begin by doing them with your legs and feet completely extended and straight out in front so that only your heels touch the floor.
- Then, work to make it a little harder by keeping your knees slightly bent and feet up off the ground.
- Finally, bend your knees more and bring your knees and legs up higher and toward your upper body.
- You might be able to only do 1, 2, or 3 reps like this at first, but each time you do it, it'll become easier (at least you'll start to get the hang of it) until you'll be able to do side-to-side seated trunk twists with your knees up high and tucked close to your body. Talk about having great balance!

Regular Seated Trunk Twist

- Do these with a broomstick or no weight at all.

- Many people who use resistance (i.e., weights) find their waistlines expanding instead of decreasing. This is simply because they're stimulating the muscles in the ab and waist area, which causes them to get bigger and thicker instead of firmer, toned, tighter, and smaller.
- You can do these either seated or standing.

- Place a broomstick behind your neck, and with both hands gripping both ends, begin twisting from side to side.
- Start off by doing slow, limited-range-of-motion twists. Increase the tempo and range of motion after one to two minutes of twisting. Do three to five minutes of continuous trunk twists.

How You Can Contact Dr. Robert Wolff

I've been surprised and overwhelmed by all the great things people all over the world have been saying since my book *Bodybuilding 101* was published. Many of you are fans from my *Muscle & Fitness* magazine days, and many others of you are new to fitness, so welcome!

Lots of people have asked how they can contact me and if there are any other things I have written that may help them? My friends, the answer is, yes! I'm happy to announce some exciting things I think you'll really like.

WWW.ROBERTWOLFF.COM

This is the official website—the one place you'll find the news on books, tips, and motivational strategies that can help change your body and your life. And fitness is only a *small* part of what you'll find.

Hot off the Press

If I Only Knew Then What I Do Now— The Lessons of Life and What They're Trying to Teach You

This is the book that I know will change your thinking and your life. Without a doubt, one of the biggest reasons my writings have been so well-received by people over the years has been the lessons I've learned from people I've met all over the world. I've been telling you, the reader, how you can learn from them—what will help you right now, today, to give you a better life and help you achieve *whatever* it is you want in your life. My passion is positive power, motivation, and learning from those who have gone through the trials and struggles of life and have reached their dreams. These are people just like you and me. Some are famous, most not so famous, but all have gone through some incredibly tough times before they reached the good times.

This book of life lessons is written for you, to inspire you and to show you many of the lessons life wants to teach you, so you too will reach your dreams, whatever they may be. You'll look forward to being inspired by this book, every day. The lessons are quick and easy to read. And the life lessons you'll learn will be the ones you need for that day, because you're the one who decides which lessons you want to learn each day. A new day, a new lesson.

That's why everyone who has read it loves this book so much—you never have to read from beginning to end. Each day, you can open to any page in the book and find something that will touch your heart and soul for that day. I call it "The Owner's Manual for Your Life."

Over the years, I've only given a few copies of it to close friends, who keep telling me to make it available to everyone because of how much they've enjoyed it and how it has inspired and changed their lives. This book has the power to change yours, too.

Visit www.RobertWolff.com often for the latest tips and inspiration you need to help you achieve the body and life you want. My friend, here's to your great success!

Index